Incredibly Easy
Chicken

Pictured on the front cover: Buffalo Chicken Salad Italiano *(page 106).*
Pictured on the back cover: Chicken and Vegetable Pasta *(page 78).*

ISBN-13: 978-1-4127-2351-0
ISBN-10: 1-4127-2351-5

Library of Congress Control Number: 2005910385

Manufactured in China.

8 7 6 5 4 3 2 1

Microwave Cooking: Microwave ovens vary in wattage. Use the cooking times as guidelines and check for doneness before adding more time.

Preparation/Cooking Times: Preparation times are based on the approximate amount of time required to assemble the recipe before cooking, baking, chilling or serving. These times include preparation steps such as measuring, chopping and mixing. The fact that some preparations and cooking can be done simultaneously is taken into account. Preparation of optional ingredients and serving suggestions is not included.

Table of Contents

Jiffy Snacks

CHICKEN WRAPS

½ teaspoon five spice powder
½ pound boneless skinless chicken thighs
½ cup bean sprouts, rinsed well and drained
2 tablespoons minced green onions, green parts only
2 tablespoons sliced almonds
2 tablespoons soy sauce
4 teaspoons hoisin sauce
1½ teaspoons hot chile sauce with garlic*
4 large leaves romaine or iceberg lettuce

Hot chile sauce with garlic is available in the Asian foods section of most supermarkets.

1. Preheat toaster oven to 350°F.

2. Sprinkle five spice powder over chicken thighs. Place on toaster oven tray. Bake 20 minutes or until chicken is no longer pink in center. Remove and dice chicken.

3. Place chicken in bowl. Add bean sprouts, onions, almonds, soy sauce, hoisin sauce and chile sauce. Stir gently but well. To serve, spoon ⅓ cup chicken mixture onto each lettuce leaf; roll or fold as desired.   *Makes 4 servings*

TORTILLA CRUNCH CHICKEN FINGERS

1 envelope LIPTON® RECIPE SECRETS® Savory Herb
    with Garlic Soup Mix
1 cup finely crushed plain tortilla chips or cornflakes
    (about 3 ounces)
1½ pounds boneless, skinless chicken breasts, cut into strips
1 egg
2 tablespoons water
2 tablespoons I CAN'T BELIEVE IT'S NOT BUTTER!® Spread, melted

1. Preheat oven to 400°F.

2. In medium bowl, combine savory herb with garlic soup mix
and tortilla chips. In large plastic bag or bowl, combine chicken
and egg beaten with water until evenly coated. Remove chicken
and dip in tortilla mixture until evenly coated; discard bag. On
15½×10½×1-inch jelly-roll pan sprayed with nonstick cooking
spray, arrange chicken; drizzle with I Can't Believe It's Not Butter!®
Spread. Bake, uncovered, 12 minutes or until chicken is thoroughly
cooked. Serve with chunky salsa, if desired.

Makes about 24 chicken fingers

BUFFALO-STYLE CHICKEN NACHOS

2 cups diced cooked chicken
⅓ cup *Frank's® RedHot®* Original Cayenne Pepper Sauce
2 tablespoons melted butter
1 bag (10 ounces) tortilla chips
3 cups shredded Cheddar or Monterey Jack cheese

1. Preheat oven to 350°F. Combine chicken, *Frank's RedHot*
Sauce and butter. Layer chips, chicken and cheese in ovenproof
serving dish or baking dish.

2. Bake 5 minutes just until cheese melts. Garnish as desired. Splash
on more *Frank's RedHot* Sauce to taste.   *Makes 4 servings*

Tortilla Crunch Chicken Fingers

Nachos con Queso y Cerveza

4 ounces tortilla chips
   Nonstick cooking spray
¾ cup chopped red onion
2 jalapeño peppers,* seeded and chopped
3 cloves garlic, finely chopped
2 teaspoons chili powder
½ teaspoon ground cumin
2 boneless skinless chicken breasts (about 8 ounces),
   cooked and chopped
1 can (14½ ounces) Mexican-style diced tomatoes, drained
⅓ cup pilsner lager
1 cup (4 ounces) shredded Monterey Jack cheese
2 tablespoons chopped pitted black olives

*Jalapeño peppers can sting and irritate the skin. Wear rubber gloves when handling peppers and do not touch eyes. Wash hands after handling peppers.

1. Preheat oven to 350°F. Place chips in 13×9-inch baking pan.

2. Spray large nonstick skillet with cooking spray. Heat over medium heat until hot. Add onion, peppers, garlic, chili powder and cumin. Cook 5 minutes or until vegetables are tender, stirring occasionally. Stir in chicken, tomatoes and lager. Simmer until liquid is absorbed.

3. Spoon chicken mixture over chips; top with cheese and olives. Bake 5 minutes or until cheese melts. Serve immediately.

Makes 4 servings

Nachos con Queso y Cerveza

CHICKEN PESTO PIZZA

Cornmeal
1 loaf (1 pound) frozen bread dough, thawed
Nonstick cooking spray
8 ounces chicken breast tenders, cut into ½-inch pieces
½ red onion, cut into quarters and thinly sliced
¼ cup prepared pesto
2 large plum tomatoes, seeded and diced
1 cup (4 ounces) shredded pizza cheese blend
    or mozzarella cheese

1. Preheat oven to 375°F. Sprinkle baking sheet with cornmeal.
Roll out bread dough on floured surface to 14×8-inch rectangle.
Transfer to prepared baking sheet. Cover loosely with plastic wrap;
let rise 20 to 30 minutes.

2. Meanwhile, spray large skillet with cooking spray; heat over
medium heat. Add chicken; cook and stir 2 minutes. Add onion
and pesto; cook and stir 3 to 4 minutes or until chicken is cooked
through. Stir in tomatoes. Remove from heat; let cool slightly.

3. Spread chicken mixture evenly over bread dough within 1 inch
of edges. Sprinkle with cheese.

4. Bake on bottom rack of oven about 20 minutes or until crust is
golden brown. Cut into 2-inch squares.

Makes about 20 appetizer pieces

FIX IT *Fast* — *When cutting boneless chicken breasts or thighs into cubes or slices, cut the chicken across the grain to make the pieces more tender.*

Chicken Pesto Pizza

BANDITO BUFFALO WINGS

1 package (1.25 ounces) ORTEGA® Taco Seasoning Mix
12 (about 1 pound *total*) chicken wings
    ORTEGA Salsa (any flavor)

PREHEAT oven to 375°F. Lightly grease 13×9-inch baking pan.

PLACE seasoning mix in heavy-duty plastic or paper bag. Add 3 chicken wings; shake well to coat. Place wings in prepared pan. Repeat until all wings have been coated.

BAKE for 35 to 40 minutes or until no longer pink near bone. Serve with salsa for dipping.   *Makes 6 appetizer servings*

CREAMY CHICKEN & ARTICHOKE QUESADILLAS

1 can (14 ounces) artichoke hearts, drained and chopped
½ cup HELLMANN'S® or BEST FOODS® Real Mayonnaise
½ cup grated Parmesan cheese
1 clove garlic, finely chopped
6 burrito-size flour tortillas
4 ounces cooked chicken, thinly sliced (about 1 cup)
½ cup shredded mozzarella cheese (about 2 ounces)

In medium bowl, combine artichokes, Hellmann's or Best Foods Real Mayonnaise, Parmesan cheese and garlic. Evenly spread mayonnaise mixture on 3 tortillas, then top with chicken, mozzarella cheese and remaining tortillas.

In 12-inch nonstick skillet sprayed with nonstick cooking spray, cook quesadillas over medium-high heat, turning once, 4 minutes or until golden brown and cheese is melted.   *Makes 3 servings*

Prep Time: 10 minutes
Cook Time: 4 minutes

Bandito Buffalo Wings

CHICKEN & VEGETABLE ROLL-UPS

4 ounces cream cheese, softened
2 tablespoons mayonnaise
1 tablespoon Dijon mustard
¼ teaspoon black pepper
3 (10- to 12-inch) flour tortillas
1 cup finely chopped cooked chicken
¾ cup shredded or finely chopped carrot
¾ cup finely chopped green bell pepper
3 tablespoons chopped green onions

1. Combine cream cheese, mayonnaise, mustard and black pepper in small bowl; stir until well blended.

2. Spread cream cheese mixture evenly onto each tortilla leaving ½-inch border. Divide chicken, carrot, bell pepper and onions evenly over cream cheese leaving 1½-inch border on cream cheese mixture at one end of each tortilla.

3. Roll up each tortilla jelly-roll fashion. Cut each roll into 1½-inch-thick slices.   *Makes 5 to 6 appetizer servings*

FIX IT
Fast

For easier slicing and better flavor, wrap the rolls in plastic wrap and refrigerate for several hours.

Chicken & Vegetable Roll-Ups

PESTO CHICKEN-FONTINA CROSTINI

1 baguette, cut into 30 (¼-inch-thick) slices
½ (16-ounce) package PERDUE® Fit 'N Easy® Thin-Sliced Skinless
    & Boneless Chicken Breast or Turkey Breast Cutlets, cut into
    30 pieces
1 tablespoon prepared pesto
¼ teaspoon red pepper flakes
6 ounces fontina cheese, cut into 30 pieces
½ cup roasted red peppers, cut into 1-inch pieces
30 small fresh basil leaves to garnish

Preheat oven to 400°F. Place baguette slices on a baking sheet and toast until golden.

Spray a nonstick skillet with olive oil cooking spray and warm over high heat. Add chicken and sauté until firm and golden. Stir in pesto and red pepper flakes. Set aside.

Place a piece of fontina on each baguette slice and return to oven until cheese melts. Top each crostini with a piece of chicken and a piece of roasted pepper. Garnish with basil leaves and serve.

Makes 30 crostini

Prep Time: 30 minutes
Cook Time: 10 minutes

FIX IT
Fast

Crostini, small slices of toasted bread, means "little toasts" in Italian. Top with any savory topping for quick-to-fix appetizers and snacks.

CHICKEN AND BLUE CHEESE ON PUMPERNICKEL

½ (16-ounce) package PERDUE® Fit 'N Easy® Thin-Sliced Skinless
   & Boneless Chicken Breast or Turkey Breast Cutlets
⅓ cup crumbled blue cheese
¾ tablespoon Dijon mustard
   Salt and pepper, to taste
16 slices cocktail pumpernickel, toasted and buttered
½ small red onion, very thinly sliced
 1 cup arugula, radicchio or watercress, very thinly sliced

Spray a large, nonstick skillet with cooking spray and warm over high heat. Sauté chicken until golden brown on both sides and cooked through. Set aside to cool.

In a medium bowl, stir together blue cheese and mustard. Dice chicken and stir it in. Season to taste with salt and pepper.

To assemble, top each slice of bread with some onion, a heaping tablespoon of chicken and sprinkle with arugula. Serve immediately.

Make 16 appetizers

Prep Time: 30 minutes
Cook Time: 5 minutes

CHICKEN TENDERS IN BACON BLANKETS

¼ **cup Dijon mustard**
¼ **cup maple syrup**
¼ **teaspoon chili powder**
4 **chicken breast tenders, cut in half lengthwise**
    (about 12 ounces)
8 **bacon strips**

1. Preheat broiler. Combine mustard, maple syrup and chili powder in medium bowl. Reserve half mustard mixture. Brush each chicken tender with remaining mustard mixture. Wrap 1 bacon strip around each chicken tender.

2. Place chicken tenders, bacon ends down, on rack of broiler pan. Broil 5 inches from heat 4 to 5 minutes on each side or until bacon is crisp and chicken is no longer pink in center. Serve with reserved mustard mixture for dipping.   *Makes 4 servings*

CHICKEN RANCH-UP!™ WRAPS

½ **cup Wish-Bone® Ranch Up!™ Classic Light, Zesty or Classic**
    Dressing
4 **(8-inch) flour tortillas**
2 **cups cut-up cooked chicken**
2 **cups vegetables, such as: red, yellow or green bell peppers, red**
    or green onion, cucumber, tomato, shredded carrots

Spread Ranch-Up!™ over tortillas, then top with remaining ingredients.

Roll up and serve.   *Makes 5 servings*

Tip: After rolling, cut the wrap on a diagonal to make 1-inch bite sized pieces.

Prep Time: 10 minutes

Chicken Tenders in Bacon Blankets

Great
Grills

THAI GRILLED CHICKEN

4 boneless skinless chicken breasts (about 1¼ pounds)
¼ cup soy sauce
2 teaspoons bottled minced garlic
½ teaspoon red pepper flakes
2 tablespoons honey
1 tablespoon fresh lime juice

1. Prepare grill for direct cooking. Place chicken in shallow baking dish. Combine soy sauce, garlic and pepper flakes in measuring cup. Pour over chicken, turning to coat. Let stand 10 minutes.

2. Meanwhile, combine honey and lime juice in small bowl until blended; set aside.

3. Place chicken on grid over medium coals; brush with marinade. Discard remaining marinade. Grill, covered, 5 minutes. Brush both sides of chicken with honey mixture. Grill 5 minutes more or until chicken is no longer pink in center. *Makes 4 servings*

Serving Suggestion: Serve with steamed white rice, Oriental vegetables and fresh fruit salad.

Prep and Cook Time: 25 minutes

CHICKEN AND FRUIT KABOBS

1¾ cups honey
¾ cup fresh lemon juice
½ cup Dijon mustard
⅓ cup chopped fresh ginger
4 pounds boneless skinless chicken breasts, cut into 1-inch chucks
6 fresh plums, pitted and quartered
3 firm bananas, cut into chunks
4 cups fresh pineapple chunks (about half of medium pineapple)

Prepare grill for direct cooking. Combine honey, lemon juice, mustard and ginger in small bowl; mix well. Thread chicken and fruit onto skewers, alternating chicken with fruit; brush generously with honey mixture. Place kabobs on grill about 4 inches from heat. Grill 5 minutes on each side, brushing frequently with honey mixture. Grill 10 minutes or until chicken is cooked through, turning and brushing frequently with remaining honey mixture. Do not baste during last 5 minutes of grilling time. Discard remaining honey mixture. *Makes 12 servings*

TEXAS SPICE RUB

1 tablespoon paprika
1 teaspoon seasoned salt
½ teaspoon brown sugar
¼ teaspoon granulated garlic
⅛ teaspoon cayenne pepper
2 teaspoons water
4 boneless skinless chicken breast halves

Combine paprika, salt, sugar, garlic and cayenne. Add water to make paste. Rub on chicken to coat evenly. Grill chicken on covered grill over medium-hot KINGSFORD® Briquets 8 to 10 minutes, turning once, until just cooked through.

Makes 4 servings

Great Grills

Chicken and Fruit Kabobs

SOUTHWEST CHICKEN

2 tablespoons olive oil
1 clove garlic, pressed
1 teaspoon ground cumin
1 teaspoon chili powder
1 teaspoon dried oregano leaves
½ teaspoon salt
1 pound skinless boneless chicken breast halves or thighs

Combine oil, garlic, cumin, chili powder, oregano and salt; brush over both sides of chicken to coat. Grill chicken over medium-hot KINGSFORD® Briquets 8 to 10 minutes or until chicken is no longer pink, turning once. Serve immediately or use in Build a Burrito, Taco Salad or other favorite recipes.   *Makes 4 servings*

Note: Southwest Chicken can be grilled ahead and refrigerated for several days or frozen for longer storage.

Build a Burrito: Top warm large flour tortillas with strips of Southwest Chicken and your choice of drained canned black beans, cooked brown or white rice, shredded cheese, salsa verde, shredded lettuce, sliced black olives and chopped cilantro. Fold in sides and roll to enclose filling. Heat in microwave oven at HIGH until heated through. (Or, wrap in foil and heat in preheated 350°F oven.)

Taco Salad: For a quick one-dish meal, layer strips of Southwest Chicken with tomato wedges, blue or traditional corn tortilla chips, sliced black olives, shredded romaine or iceberg lettuce, shredded cheese and avocado slices. Serve with salsa, sour cream, guacamole or a favorite dressing.

Southwest Chicken

57 & HONEY GLAZED KABOBS

⅔ cup **HEINZ 57 Sauce®**
⅓ cup **honey**
4 **skinless boneless chicken breast halves, each cut into 8 cubes (about 1 pound)**
Fresh vegetables, cut into 1½ inch pieces (such as onions, mushrooms, bell peppers, zucchini and yellow squash)
Cooking spray

Combine 57 Sauce and honey; set aside. Alternately thread chicken and vegetables on skewers. Spray with cooking spray. Grill over medium heat 12 to 15 minutes, turning often, until chicken is cooked. Brush liberally with 57 Sauce mixture. Grill until kabobs are brown and glazed, about 5 minutes.   *Makes 4 servings*

FAJITA-SEASONED GRILLED CHICKEN

4 **boneless skinless chicken breasts (about 4 ounces each)**
2 **bunches green onions, ends trimmed**
2 **tablespoons olive oil**
4 **teaspoons fajita seasoning mix**

1. Prepare grill for direct cooking.

2. Brush chicken and green onions with oil. Sprinkle both sides of chicken breasts with seasoning mix. Grill chicken and onions 6 to 8 minutes or until chicken is no longer pink in center.

3. Serve chicken with onions.   *Makes 4 servings*

57 & Honey Glazed Kabobs

BLUE CHEESE STUFFED CHICKEN BREASTS

½ **cup (2 ounces) crumbled blue cheese**
2 **tablespoons butter, softened, divided**
¾ **teaspoon dried thyme**
   Salt
   Black pepper
2 **whole boneless chicken breasts with skin (not split)**
1 **tablespoon lemon juice**
½ **teaspoon paprika**

1. Prepare grill for direct cooking. Combine blue cheese, 1 tablespoon butter and thyme in small bowl until blended. Season with salt and pepper.

2. Loosen skin over breast of chicken by pushing fingers between skin and meat, taking care not to tear skin. Spread blue cheese mixture under skin with rubber spatula or small spoon; massage skin to evenly spread cheese mixture.

3. Place chicken, skin side down, on grid over medium coals. Grill, covered, 5 minutes. Meanwhile, melt remaining 1 tablespoon butter; stir in lemon juice and paprika. Turn chicken; brush with lemon juice mixture. Grill 5 to 7 minutes more or until chicken is no longer pink in center. Transfer chicken to carving board; cut each breast in half.   *Makes 4 servings*

Serving Suggestion: Serve with steamed new potatoes and broccoli.

Prep and Cook Time: 22 minutes

Blue Cheese Stuffed Chicken Breast

GRILLED CHICKEN
WITH CHIMICHURRI SALSA

4 boneless skinless chicken breasts (6 ounces each)
½ cup plus 4 teaspoons olive oil
   Salt and black pepper
½ cup finely chopped parsley
¼ cup white wine vinegar
2 tablespoons finely chopped onion
3 cloves garlic, minced
1 fresh or canned jalapeño pepper, finely chopped
2 teaspoons dried oregano

1. Prepare grill for direct cooking.

2. Brush chicken with 4 teaspoons olive oil; season with salt and black pepper. Place on oiled grid. Grill, covered, over medium heat 5 to 8 minutes on each side or until chicken is no longer pink in center.

3. To prepare sauce, combine parsley, remaining ½ cup olive oil, vinegar, onion, garlic, jalapeño pepper, oregano and salt and black pepper to taste. Serve over chicken.   *Makes 4 servings*

FIX IT
Fast

Chimichurri salsa has a fresh, green color. Serve it with grilled steak or fish as well as chicken. Chimichurri will remain fresh tasting for 24 hours.

GRILLED CHICKEN STIX

1 pound thin sliced chicken breast cutlets
12 to 14 wooden skewers, soaked in water
2 oranges, cut into eighths
½ cup barbecue sauce
½ cup honey
3 tablespoons *Frank's® RedHot®* Original Cayenne Pepper Sauce
Spicy Cucumber Salsa (recipe follows)

1. Slice cutlets into ½-inch-wide long strips. Weave strips onto upper half of 8 to 10 skewers. Place skewers into large baking dish. Thread 4 orange pieces each onto remaining 4 skewers. Set aside.

2. Combine barbecue sauce, honey and *Frank's RedHot* Sauce in measuring cup. Reserve ¼ cup sauce for Spicy Cucumber Salsa. Pour ½ cup of remaining mixture over chicken, turning skewers to coat.

3. Grill or broil chicken and orange skewers 5 minutes or until chicken is no longer pink in center and oranges are heated through. Turn and baste often with remaining sauce. Serve with Spicy Cucumber Salsa. *Makes 4 servings*

SPICY CUCUMBER SALSA

1 large cucumber, peeled, seeded and chopped
1 small red bell pepper, finely chopped
¼ cup finely chopped red onion
2 tablespoons finely chopped fresh cilantro or parsley
Reserved ¼ cup barbecue sauce mixture

Combine all ingredients in large bowl; chill. Serve with Grilled Chicken Stix or your favorite grilled chicken or steak recipe.
Makes 4 to 6 servings (about 2 cups)

GRILLED ROSEMARY CHICKEN

2 tablespoons minced fresh rosemary
2 tablespoons lemon juice
2 tablespoons olive oil
2 cloves garlic, minced
¼ teaspoon salt
4 boneless skinless chicken breasts (about 1 pound)

1. Spray cold grid of grill with nonstick cooking spray. Prepare grill for direct cooking.

2. Whisk together rosemary, lemon juice, oil, garlic and salt in small bowl. Pour into shallow glass dish. Add chicken, turning to coat both sides with lemon juice mixture. Cover; marinate in refrigerator 15 minutes, turning chicken once. Remove chicken; discard marinade.

3. Grill chicken over medium-hot coals 5 to 6 minutes per side or until chicken is no longer pink in center. Serve with grilled or steamed fresh vegetables; if desired. *Makes 4 servings*

Prep and Cook Time: 30 minutes

FIX IT
Fast

To add more flavor to the chicken, moisten a few sprigs of fresh rosemary and toss on the hot coals just before grilling. To store fresh rosemary, wrap sprigs in a barely damp paper towel and place in a sealed plastic bag. It can be kept in the refrigerator for up to five days.

Grilled Rosemary Chicken

GRILLED GINGER CHICKEN WITH PINEAPPLE AND COCONUT RICE

1 can (20 ounces) pineapple rings in juice
⅔ cup uncooked white rice
½ cup unsweetened flaked coconut
4 boneless skinless chicken breasts (about 1 pound)
1 tablespoon soy sauce
1 teaspoon ground ginger

1. Drain juice from pineapple into glass measuring cup. Reserve 2 tablespoons juice. Combine remaining juice with enough water to equal 2 cups.

2. Cook and stir rice and coconut in medium saucepan over medium heat 3 to 4 minutes or until lightly browned. Add juice mixture; cover and bring to a boil. Reduce heat to low; cook 15 minutes or until rice is tender and liquid is absorbed.

3. While rice is cooking, combine chicken, reserved 2 tablespoons juice, soy sauce and ginger in medium bowl; toss well.

4. Grill or broil chicken 6 minutes; turn. Add pineapple to grill or broiler pan. Cook 6 to 8 minutes or until chicken is no longer pink in center, turning pineapple after 3 minutes.

5. Transfer rice to four serving plates; serve with chicken and pineapple. *Makes 4 servings*

Prep and Cook Time: 22 minutes

Grilled Ginger Chicken with Pineapple and Coconut Rice

GRILLED GARLIC CHICKEN

**1 envelope LIPTON® RECIPE SECRETS® Savory Herb with Garlic
    Soup Mix**
3 tablespoons BERTOLLI® Olive Oil
4 boneless, skinless chicken breast halves (about 1¼ pounds)

1. In medium bowl, combine soup mix with oil.

2. Add chicken; toss to coat.

3. Grill or broil until chicken is thoroughly cooked.

Makes 4 servings

LEMON-GARLIC CHICKEN

2 tablespoons olive oil
2 cloves garlic, pressed
1 teaspoon grated lemon peel
1 teaspoon lemon juice
¼ teaspoon salt
¼ teaspoon black pepper
4 skinless boneless chicken breast halves (about 1 pound)

Combine oil, garlic, lemon peel, lemon juice, salt and pepper in
small bowl. Brush oil mixture over both sides of chicken to coat.
Lightly oil grid to prevent sticking. Grill chicken over medium
KINGSFORD® Briquets 8 to 10 minutes or until chicken is no
longer pink in center, turning once.   *Makes 4 servings*

Grilled Garlic Chicken

GRILLED TUSCAN CHICKEN SANDWICH

4 boneless skinless chicken breast halves
2 tablespoons olive oil
2 tablespoons MRS. DASH® Tomato Basil Garlic Seasoning
½ cup sliced green olives
½ cup light mayonnaise
4 large crusty rolls
4 slices roasted red peppers, from a jar or deli counter
4 large romaine lettuce leaves, washed and patted dry, torn
    in half crosswise

Preheat grill to medium-high. Brush chicken breasts with olive oil on each side and sprinkle with Mrs. Dash® Tomato Basil Garlic seasoning. Grill for 5 minutes, turn, and grill for another 5 minutes, or until juices run clear when a skewer is inserted. Remove and cool slightly. In a bowl, mix sliced olives and mayonnaise. Cut rolls in half and spread the olive mixture on each side of each roll. Layer lettuce leaf half, chicken breast, roasted red pepper slice and other half of lettuce leaf on each of bottom roll half, and place other half of roll on top. Serve immediately.   *Makes 4 servings*

Prep Time: 10 minutes
Cooking Time: 12 minutes

FIX IT Fast

To check the doneness of grilled chicken, cut a slit into the thickest part. The appearance of the meat should look opaque not pink and the juices should run clear. Or, insert an instant read thermometer horizontally into the thickest part of the thigh or breast. The temperature should reach 170°F.

ITALIAN CHICKEN KABOBS

½ cup Italian salad dressing
¼ cup chopped fresh basil leaves
1 medium yellow onion, peeled
1 medium red bell pepper, seeded
1 medium zucchini, scrubbed
1 small jicama, peeled
1 package (about 1 pound) PERDUE® Fresh Italian Seasoned
    Boneless Chicken Breasts

In large bowl, combine Italian dressing with basil. Cut vegetables into chunks; place in dressing. Cover and marinate 1 to 2 hours.

Prepare grill for cooking. Cut chicken into 1½-inch chunks. On metal skewers, thread chicken chunks, alternating with marinated vegetables, until all ingredients are used. Grill kabobs over medium-hot coals 10 to 15 minutes, until chicken is cooked through, turning occasionally.   *Makes 4 servings*

CAJUN GRILLED CHICKEN

4 boneless skinless chicken breast halves
2 tablespoons lemon juice
3 tablespoons MRS. DASH® Extra Spicy Seasoning
2 tablespoons paprika
1 tablespoon brown sugar
    Cooking spray

Preheat grill to medium-high. With a sharp knife, slash each piece of chicken in 2 or 3 places with ¼-inch-deep cuts. In a bowl, combine chicken and lemon juice, turning the chicken until it is thoroughly coated. Set aside. In separate bowl, mix Mrs. Dash® Extra Spicy Seasoning, paprika and brown sugar. Take each piece of chicken and roll in the spice mixture until well coated. Spray grill with cooking spray and place seasoned chicken breasts on the grill. Cook 5 minutes and turn. Cook 5 minutes more or until juices run clear when a skewer is inserted. Serve immediately.   *Makes 4 servings*

Easy Dinners

MONTEREY CHICKEN AND RICE QUICHE

4 boneless, skinless chicken tenderloins, cut into 1-inch pieces
1¾ cups water
1 box UNCLE BEN'S® COUNTRY INN® Chicken
    & Vegetable Rice
1 cup frozen mixed vegetables
1 (9-inch) deep-dish ready-to-use frozen pie crust
3 eggs
½ cup milk
½ cup (2 ounces) shredded Monterey Jack cheese

1. Heat oven to 400°F.

2. In large skillet, combine chicken, water, rice, contents of seasoning packet and frozen vegetables. Bring to a boil. Cover; reduce heat and simmer 10 minutes. Spoon mixture into pie crust.

3. In small bowl, beat eggs and milk. Pour over rice mixture in pie crust; top with cheese. Bake 30 to 35 minutes or until knife inserted in center comes out clean.   *Makes 6 servings*

Serving Suggestion: A fresh fruit compote of orange sections and green grapes or blueberries is the perfect accompaniment to this delicious quiche.

RANCH BAKED QUESADILLAS

1 cup shredded cooked chicken
1 cup (4 ounces) shredded Monterey Jack cheese
½ cup HIDDEN VALLEY® The Original Ranch® Dressing
¼ cup diced green chiles, rinsed and drained
4 (9-inch) flour tortillas, heated
Salsa and guacamole (optional)

Combine chicken, cheese, dressing and chiles in a medium bowl.
Place about ½ cup chicken mixture on each tortilla; fold in half.
Place quesadillas on a baking sheet. Bake at 350°F. for 15 minutes
or until cheese is melted. Cut into thirds, if desired. Serve with salsa
and guacamole, if desired.   *Makes 4 servings*

SNAPPY SOUTHWEST CHICKEN

2 cans (10 ounces each) tomatoes and green chilies
1 cup diced zucchini
1 can (7 ounces) whole kernel corn, drained
1 tablespoon chili powder
1⅓ cups *French's*® French Fried Onions, divided
4 boneless skinless chicken breast halves
Cooked white rice (optional)

Preheat oven to 400°F. Combine tomatoes and green chilies,
zucchini, corn, chili powder and ⅔ cup French Fried Onions in
2-quart oblong baking dish. Arrange chicken over tomato mixture.
Spoon a few tablespoons of mixture over chicken.

Bake, uncovered, 30 minutes or until chicken is no longer pink
in center. Stir vegetables around chicken. Sprinkle chicken with
remaining ⅔ *cup* onions. Bake 1 minute or until onions are golden.
Serve with rice, if desired.   *Makes 4 servings*

Prep Time: 5 minutes
Cook Time: 31 minutes

Ranch Baked Quesadillas

PESTO-COATED BAKED CHICKEN

1 pound boneless skinless chicken breasts,
    cut into ½-inch-thick cutlets
¼ cup plus 1 tablespoon prepared pesto
1½ teaspoons sour cream
1½ teaspoons mayonnaise
1 tablespoon shredded Parmesan cheese
1 tablespoon pine nuts

1. Preheat oven to 450°F. Arrange chicken in single layer in shallow baking pan. Combine pesto, sour cream and mayonnaise in small cup. Brush over chicken. Sprinkle with cheese and pine nuts.

2. Bake 8 to 10 minutes or until chicken is no longer pink in center. *Makes 4 servings*

Variation: Chicken can be cooked on an oiled grid over a preheated grill.

FIX IT *Fast*

Pesto is Italian for "pounded." It's an uncooked sauce made from fresh basil, garlic, pine nuts, olive oil and Parmesan cheese. Use flavorful pesto to make another quick dinner. Slice leftover baked chicken and toss it with whole wheat pasta, fresh veggies, olive oil and a little pesto for a yummy pasta salad.

Pesto-Coated Baked Chicken

EASY CHICKEN CHALUPAS

1 fully cooked rotisserie chicken (about 2 pounds)
8 flour tortillas
2 cups shredded Cheddar cheese
1 cup mild green chili salsa
1 cup mild red salsa

1. Preheat oven to 350°F. Spray 13×9-inch ovenproof dish with nonstick cooking spray.

2. Remove skin and bones from chicken; discard. Shred chicken meat.

3. Place 2 tortillas in bottom of prepared dish, overlapping slightly. Layer tortillas with 1 cup chicken, ½ cup cheese and ¼ cup of each salsa. Repeat layers, ending with cheese and salsas.

4. Bake casserole 25 minutes or until bubbly and hot.

Makes 6 servings

FIX IT *Fast*

Serve this easy main dish with toppings on the side such as sour cream, chopped cilantro, sliced black olives, sliced green onions and sliced avocado.

Easy Chicken Chalupas

CHICKEN DIVAN

1 package (10 ounces) frozen broccoli spears, thawed
   and drained
1½ cups cooked unsalted regular rice (½ cup uncooked)
1⅓ cups *French's®* French Fried Onions, divided
1 can (10¾ ounces) condensed cream of chicken soup
½ cup sour cream
½ cup (2 ounces) shredded Cheddar cheese
1 teaspoon paprika
¼ teaspoon curry powder (optional)
1 cup (5 ounces) cubed cooked chicken

Preheat oven to 350°F. In 10-inch pie plate, arrange broccoli spears with flowerets around edge of dish. (It may be necessary to halve stalks to obtain enough flowerets.) To hot rice in saucepan, add ⅔ *cup* French Fried Onions, soup, sour cream, cheese, seasonings and chicken; stir well. Spoon chicken mixture evenly over broccoli stalks. Bake, covered, at 350°F for 30 minutes or until heated through. Top with remaining ⅔ *cup* onions; bake, uncovered, 5 minutes or until onions are golden brown.

Makes 4 servings

FIX IT *Fast*

While this delicious one-dish meal is in the oven, prepare a salad from prewashed greens and your favorite salad dressing. Wrap bread or rolls in foil; then, warm in the oven the last 10 minutes of cooking. A complete nutritious meal will be on the table in a hurry.

SOUTHERN BUTTERMILK FRIED CHICKEN

3 pounds chicken pieces
2 cups all-purpose flour
1½ teaspoons celery salt
1 teaspoon dried thyme
¾ teaspoon black pepper
½ teaspoon dried marjoram
1¾ cups buttermilk
2 cups vegetable oil

1. Rinse chicken; pat dry with paper towels. Combine flour, celery salt, thyme, pepper and marjoram in shallow bowl. Pour buttermilk into medium bowl.

2. Heat oil in large skillet* over medium heat until oil reaches 340°F on deep-fat thermometer.

3. Dip half the chicken in buttermilk, one piece at a time; shake off excess buttermilk. Coat with flour mixture; shake off excess. Dip again in buttermilk, then coat with flour mixture. Fry chicken, skin side down, 10 to 12 minutes or until brown; turn and fry 12 to 14 minutes or until brown and chicken is no longer pink in center. Drain on paper towels. Repeat with remaining chicken, buttermilk and flour mixture. *Makes 4 servings*

A cast iron skillet or a heavy deep skillet are good choices for pan-frying.

FIX IT *Fast*

Carefully monitor the temperature of the vegetable oil during cooking. It should not drop below 325°F or go higher than 350°F. Chicken may also be cooked in a deep fryer following the manufacturer's directions. Never leave hot oil unattended.

CHICKEN AND ASPARAGUS STIR-FRY

1 cup uncooked rice
2 tablespoons vegetable oil
1 pound boneless skinless chicken breasts, cut into
    ½-inch-wide strips
2 medium red bell peppers, cut into thin strips
½ pound fresh asparagus,* cut diagonally into 1-inch pieces
½ cup stir-fry sauce

*For stir-frying, select thin stalks of asparagus to cook more quickly.

1. Cook rice according to package directions. Keep hot.

2. Heat oil in wok or large skillet over medium-high heat until hot. Stir-fry chicken 3 to 4 minutes or until chicken is cooked through.

3. Stir in bell peppers and asparagus; reduce heat to medium. Cover; cook 2 minutes or until vegetables are crisp-tender, stirring once or twice.

4. Stir in sauce. Serve immediately with rice.   *Makes 4 servings*

Prep and Cook Time: 18 minutes

Chicken and Asparagus Stir-Fry

SAUCY TOMATO CHICKEN

6 ounces uncooked egg noodles
1 can (14½ ounces) stewed tomatoes with onions, celery
    and green bell pepper
2 cloves garlic, minced
1 teaspoon dried oregano
   Nonstick cooking spray
4 boneless skinless chicken breasts (4 ounces each)
2 teaspoons olive oil

1. Cook noodles according to package directions; drain.

2. Meanwhile, add tomatoes, garlic and oregano to large nonstick skillet. Bring to a boil over high heat; boil 5 minutes, stirring constantly, or until liquid is reduced and tomato mixture becomes slightly darker in color. (Mixture will be thick.) Transfer to small bowl; keep warm. Wipe out skillet.

3. Spray same skillet with cooking spray. Add chicken; cook 6 minutes. Turn; reduce heat to medium-low. Spoon tomato mixture into skillet around chicken. Cover; cook 4 minutes or until chicken is no longer pink in center.

4. Place noodles on serving platter; top with chicken pieces. Add olive oil to tomato mixture; stir well to blend. Spoon equal amounts of tomato mixture over each piece of chicken. *Makes 4 servings*

Saucy Tomato Chicken

CHICKEN PARMESAN

4 boneless, skinless chicken breast halves
2 cans (14½ ounces each) DEL MONTE® Stewed
Tomatoes - Italian Recipe
2 tablespoons cornstarch
½ teaspoon dried oregano or basil, crushed
¼ teaspoon hot pepper sauce (optional)
¼ cup grated Parmesan cheese
Hot cooked rice (optional)

1. Preheat oven to 425°F. Slightly flatten each chicken breast; place in 11×7-inch baking dish.

2. Cover with foil; bake 20 minutes or until chicken is no longer pink. Remove foil; drain.

3. Meanwhile, in large saucepan, combine tomatoes, cornstarch, oregano and pepper sauce, if desired. Stir to dissolve cornstarch. Cook, stirring constantly, until thickened.

4. Pour sauce over chicken; top with cheese.

5. Return to oven; bake, uncovered, 5 minutes or until cheese is melted. Garnish with chopped parsley and serve with rice or pasta, if desired. *Makes 4 servings*

Prep and Cook Time: 30 minutes

Chicken Parmesan

BROCCOLI, CHICKEN AND RICE CASSEROLE

**1 box UNCLE BEN'S COUNTRY INN® Broccoli Rice Au Gratin
    Supreme**
2 cups boiling water
4 boneless, skinless chicken breasts (about 1 pound)
¼ teaspoon garlic powder
2 cups frozen broccoli
1 cup (4 ounces) reduced-fat shredded Cheddar cheese

1. Heat oven to 425°F. In 13×9-inch baking pan, combine rice and contents of seasoning packet. Add boiling water; mix well. Add chicken; sprinkle with garlic powder. Cover and bake 30 minutes.

2. Add broccoli and cheese; continue to bake, covered, 8 to 10 minutes or until chicken is no longer pink in center.

Makes 4 servings

FLORENTINE CHICKEN

2 boxes (10 ounces each) BIRDS EYE® frozen Chopped Spinach
1 package (1.25 ounces) hollandaise sauce mix
½ teaspoon TABASCO®* Pepper Sauce or to taste
⅓ cup shredded Cheddar cheese, divided
1½ cups cubed cooked chicken

*Tabasco® is a registered trademark of McIlhenny Company.

Preheat oven to 350°F.

Cook spinach according to package directions; drain. Prepare hollandaise sauce according to package directions.

Blend spinach, hollandaise sauce, Tabasco sauce and half of cheese. Pour into 9×9-inch baking dish; top with chicken.

Sprinkle remaining cheese on top. Bake 10 to 12 minutes or until heated through. *Makes 4 servings*

Prep Time: 2 minutes
Cook Time: 10 to 12 minutes

Broccoli, Chicken and Rice Casserole

SAVORY DILL CHICKEN

2 tablespoons I CAN'T BELIEVE IT'S NOT BUTTER!® Spread
1½ pounds boneless, skinless chicken breast halves
   1 cup water
   1 package KNORR® Recipe Classics™ Vegetable or Spring
      Vegetable Soup, Dip and Recipe Mix
  ¼ teaspoon dried dill weed
  ½ cup sour cream

• In large skillet, melt I Can't Believe It's Not Butter!® Spread over medium-high heat and brown chicken, turning occasionally, 5 minutes.

• Stir in water, recipe mix and dill weed. Bring to a boil over high heat. Reduce heat to low and simmer covered, stirring occasionally, 10 minutes or until chicken is thoroughly cooked. Remove chicken to serving platter and keep warm.

• Remove skillet from heat; stir in sour cream. Spoon sauce over chicken and serve, if desired, with noodles.

Makes 4 to 6 servings

Prep Time: 5 minutes
Cook Time: 16 minutes

FIX IT *Fast*

Substitute boneless skinless chicken thighs for boneless skinless chicken breasts. Chicken thighs cook in the same amount of time, have a wonderful flavor and are a great value.

Savory Dill Chicken

CHICKEN AND RICE PUFFS

1 box frozen puff pastry shells, thawed

1 package (about 6 ounces) long grain and wild rice

2 cups cubed cooked chicken

½ can (10¾ ounces) condensed cream of chicken soup, undiluted

⅓ cup chopped slivered almonds, toasted*

⅓ cup diced celery

⅓ cup diced red bell pepper

⅓ cup chopped fresh parsley

¼ cup diced onion

¼ cup white wine or chicken broth

2 tablespoons half-and-half (optional)

*To toast almonds, spread in single layer on baking sheet. Bake in preheated 350°F oven 8 to 10 minutes or until golden brown, stirring frequently.

1. Bake pastry shells according to package directions. Keep warm.

2. Prepare rice according to package directions.

3. Add remaining ingredients to rice; mix well. Cook over medium heat 4 to 5 minutes or until hot and bubbly. Fill pastry shells with rice mixture. Serve immediately.   *Makes 6 servings*

FIX IT
Fast

Cooked chicken is a terrific timesaver when preparing meals in a hurry. Either skin and bone a rotisserie chicken, double a recipe to make extra cooked chicken, or purchase fully cooked chicken pieces or strips in the refrigerated section of the meat case.

Chicken and Rice Puff

TERIYAKI CHICKEN MEDLEY

2 cups cooked white rice (about ¾ cup uncooked)
2 cups (10 ounces) cooked chicken, cut into strips
1⅓ cups *French's*® French Fried Onions, divided
1 package (12 ounces) frozen bell pepper strips, thawed and drained*
1 jar (12 ounces) chicken gravy
3 tablespoons teriyaki sauce

*Or, substitute 2 cups sliced bell peppers for frozen pepper strips.

Preheat oven to 400°F. Grease 2-quart oblong baking dish. Press rice onto bottom of prepared dish.

Combine chicken, *⅔ cup* French Fried Onions, bell pepper strips, gravy and teriyaki sauce in large bowl; mix well. Pour mixture over rice layer. Cover; bake 30 minutes or until heated through. Top with remaining *⅔ cup* onions. Bake 1 minute or until onions are golden brown. *Makes 4 to 6 servings*

Prep Time: 10 minutes
Cook Time: 31 minutes

BROILED LEMON CHICKEN

4 skinless boneless chicken breast halves (about 1 pound)
¼ cup HEINZ® Worcestershire Sauce
2 tablespoons lemon juice
1 teaspoon minced garlic
½ teaspoon pepper
½ teaspoon grated lemon peel
   Vegetable oil

Lightly flatten chicken breasts to uniform thickness. For marinade, combine Worcestershire sauce and next 4 ingredients; pour over chicken. Cover; marinate 30 minutes, turning once. Place chicken on broiler pan, brush with oil; broil 3 to 4 minutes on each side. *Makes 4 servings*

Teriyaki Chicken Medley

CHICKEN PUTTANESCA-STYLE

2 tablespoons olive oil
1 (2½- to 3-pound) chicken, cut into pieces
1 medium onion, sliced
¼ cup balsamic vinegar
1 jar (1 pound 10 ounces) RAGÚ® Old World Style® Pasta Sauce
1 cup pitted ripe olives
1 tablespoon drained capers

In 12-inch skillet, heat olive oil over medium-high heat and brown chicken. Remove chicken and set aside; drain.

In same skillet, add onion and vinegar and cook over medium heat, stirring occasionally, 3 minutes. Stir in Ragú Old World Style Pasta Sauce. Return chicken to skillet and simmer covered 25 minutes or until chicken is thoroughly cooked. Stir in olives and capers; heat through. Serve, if desired, over hot cooked rice and garnish with chopped fresh parsley.   *Makes 4 servings*

FIX IT *Fast*   *Be sure to use the best quality balsamic vinegar you can afford. In general, the longer it's been aged, the deeper and tastier the flavor.*

Chicken Puttanesca-Style

CHICKEN BREASTS SMOTHERED IN TOMATOES AND MOZZARELLA

4 boneless skinless chicken breasts (about 1½ pounds)
3 tablespoons olive oil, divided
1 cup chopped onions
2 teaspoons minced garlic
1 can (14½ ounces) Italian-style stewed tomatoes
1½ cups (6 ounces) shredded mozzarella cheese

1. Preheat broiler.

2. Pound chicken breasts between 2 pieces of plastic wrap to ¼-inch thickness using flat side of meat mallet or rolling pin.

3. Heat 2 tablespoons oil in ovenproof skillet over medium heat. Add chicken; cook about 3½ minutes per side or until no longer pink in center. Transfer to plate; cover and keep warm.

4. Heat remaining 1 tablespoon oil in same skillet over medium heat. Add onions and garlic; cook and stir 3 minutes. Add tomatoes; bring to a simmer. Return chicken to skillet, spooning onion and tomato mixture over chicken.

5. Sprinkle cheese over top. Broil 4 to 5 inches from heat until cheese is melted.   *Makes 4 servings*

Prep and Cook Time: 20 minutes

Chicken Breast Smothered in Tomatoes and Mozzarella

CHILI CRANBERRY CHICKEN

½ cup **HEINZ® Chili Sauce**
½ cup **whole berry cranberry sauce**
 2 tablespoons **orange marmalade**
⅛ teaspoon **ground allspice**
 4 to 6 **skinless boneless chicken breast halves (about 1½ pounds)**
 2 teaspoons **vegetable oil**

Combine first 4 ingredients; set aside. In large skillet, slowly brown chicken on both sides in oil. Pour reserved chili sauce mixture over chicken. Simmer, uncovered, 8 to 10 minutes or until chicken is cooked and sauce is of desired consistency, turning and basting occasionally. *Makes 4 to 6 servings and about 1 cup sauce*

FIX IT
Fast

Stock your freezer with individually quick-frozen boneless chicken breasts. They can be conveniently used one or two at a time. Because they are in single pieces instead of a frozen block, they defrost quickly in the microwave.

Chili Cranberry Chicken

CHICKEN PICANTE

½ cup medium-hot chunky taco sauce
¼ cup Dijon mustard
   Juice of 1 medium lime
6 boneless skinless chicken breasts
2 tablespoons butter
   Plain yogurt
   Chopped fresh cilantro and lime slices for garnish

1. Combine taco sauce, mustard and lime juice in large bowl. Add chicken, turning to coat with marinade. Cover; marinate in refrigerator at least 30 minutes.

2. Melt butter in large skillet over medium heat until foamy.

3. Drain chicken, reserving marinade. Add chicken to skillet in single layer. Cook 10 minutes or until chicken is light brown on both sides. Add reserved marinade to skillet; cook 5 minutes or until chicken is no longer pink in center and glazed with marinade.

4. Remove chicken to serving platter; keep warm. Boil marinade in skillet over high heat 1 minute; pour over chicken. Serve with yogurt. Garnish with cilantro and lime.   *Makes 6 servings*

FIX IT
Fast

For easy chicken meals later in the week, double this recipe. Cut up chicken for a pasta salad or a fast casserole. Or, top a taco salad with the cut up chicken.

Chicken Picante

Orange Pecan Chicken

1 cup orange juice
¼ cup vegetable oil
   Salt and black pepper
4 boneless skinless chicken breasts
   Orange Pecan Sauce (recipe follows)

1. In medium bowl, whisk together juice and oil until well blended. Add salt and pepper to taste. Place chicken breasts in 9×9-inch baking pan or resealable food storage bag. Pour juice mixture over chicken. If using baking pan, cover with plastic wrap. If using bag, seal securely. Marinate in refrigerator 30 minutes.

2. Meanwhile, prepare Orange Pecan Sauce.

3. Preheat broiler. Remove chicken from pan or bag; discard marinade. Broil chicken about 6 to 8 minutes on each side or until no longer pink in center, turning once. Serve with Orange Pecan Sauce. *Makes 4 servings*

Orange Pecan Sauce

⅓ cup frozen orange juice concentrate, thawed
⅓ cup butter or margarine
2 tablespoons teriyaki sauce
1 clove garlic, minced
2 tablespoons packed dark brown sugar
2 tablespoons chopped toasted pecans
   Dash ground red pepper

Combine orange juice, butter, teriyaki sauce and garlic in small saucepan. Bring to a simmer over medium heat. Cook and stir 2 to 3 minutes or until well blended. Add brown sugar. Cook and stir 4 to 5 minutes or until sauce is slightly thickened. Remove from heat. Stir in pecans and red pepper. Serve warm or at room temperature over chicken. *Makes about 1 cup*

Orange Pecan Chicken

MUSTARD CHICKEN

1 large or 2 small broiling chickens,
    cut into serving pieces and skinned
Freshly ground pepper
½ cup prepared mustard*
2 tablespoons brown sugar
1 clove garlic, minced
½ teaspoon dry mustard
Dry bread crumbs

*Can substitute ¼ cup prepared mustard and ¼ cup Dijon mustard.

Preheat oven to 400°F. Sprinkle chicken pieces with pepper; place on rack in roasting pan and bake until lightly golden, 10 to 15 minutes.

Combine prepared mustard, sugar, garlic and dry mustard; blend well. Brush both sides of chicken pieces with mustard mixture. Roll in bread crumbs, coating lightly. Return to rack and bake 20 minutes. Turn pieces over and bake another 30 minutes, or until chicken is tender and coating is crusty.   *Makes 4 to 6 servings*

Favorite recipe from **The Sugar Association, Inc.**

FIX IT
Fast

To save preparation time, purchase cut up instead of whole chickens. To save clean-up time, line the roasting pans with foil. To save energy, cook the complete meal in the oven. Roast vegetables in another baking pan for a simple supper from the oven.

Mustard Chicken

ONION CRUMB
CHICKEN CUTLETS

1⅓ cups *French's®* French Fried Onions
4 thinly sliced chicken cutlets (1 pound), pounded to ¼-inch
   thickness
3 tablespoons *French's®* Bold n' Spicy Brown Mustard
1 to 2 tablespoons vegetable oil
   Salt and pepper to taste

Place French Fried Onions in resealable plastic food storage bag; seal. Press with rolling pin until onions are finely crushed. Transfer to sheet of waxed paper.

Brush each side of chicken with about 1 teaspoon mustard. Dip into crushed onions; pressing gently to coat.

Heat 1 tablespoon oil in large nonstick skillet over medium heat. Cook chicken, in batches, 1 to 2 minutes per side or until no longer pink in center. Repeat with remaining oil and cutlets. Season to taste with salt and pepper.   *Makes 4 servings*

Prep Time: 15 minutes
Cook Time: 4 to 8 minutes

 FIX IT

When cooking or browning chicken parts or pieces, do not put too many pieces in the skillet at one time. Leave space between the pieces to allow them to brown and cook more evenly.

CHILI-CORN CRUSTED CHICKEN

4 boneless, skinless chicken breast halves
¼ cup low-fat milk
½ cup cornmeal
½ teaspoon salt
1 teaspoon chili powder
3 tablespoons vegetable oil
Salsa (optional)

With meat mallet or similar utensil, pound chicken to ¼-inch thickness. In shallow dish, place milk. In second shallow dish, mix together cornmeal, salt, and chili powder. Dip chicken, one piece at a time, in milk, then in cornmeal mixture, turning to coat on all sides. In large nonstick skillet, place oil and heat to medium-high temperature. Add chicken and cook, turning, about 8 to 10 minutes or until chicken is brown and fork tender. Serve with your choice of prepared salsa, if desired. *Makes 4 servings*

Favorite recipe from Delmarva Poultry Industry, Inc.

CHICKEN POMODORO WITH TOMATO BASIL GARLIC

4 teaspoons olive oil
8 boneless skinless chicken breast halves
8 ounces fresh mushrooms, sliced
2 cans (14¼ ounces each) Italian-style stewed tomatoes
8 teaspoons MRS. DASH® Tomato Basil Garlic Seasoning
½ cup semi-dry white wine (optional)

Heat oil in nonstick skillet. Add chicken and brown over medium heat about 10 minutes, turning once. Add remaining ingredients. Bring to a boil; reduce heat and simmer, uncovered, 15 minutes.

Makes 8 servings

Prep Time: 10 minutes
Cook Time: 25 minutes

Quick Pastas

CHICKEN AND VEGETABLE PASTA

8 ounces (4 cups) uncooked bowtie pasta
2 red or green bell peppers, cut into quarters
1 medium zucchini, cut into halves
3 boneless skinless chicken breasts (about ¾ pound)
½ cup Italian dressing
½ cup prepared pesto sauce

1. Cook pasta according to package directions. Drain; place in large bowl. Cover to keep warm.

2. While pasta is cooking, combine vegetables, chicken and dressing in medium bowl; toss well. Grill or broil 6 to 8 minutes on each side or until vegetables are crisp-tender and chicken is no longer pink in center. (Vegetables may take less time than chicken.)

3. Cut vegetables and chicken into bite-size pieces. Add vegetables, chicken and pesto to pasta; toss well.

Makes 4 to 6 servings

Prep and Cook Time: 20 minutes

Spicy Mesquite Chicken Fettuccine

8 ounces uncooked fettuccine
1 tablespoon chili powder
1 teaspoon ground cumin
1 teaspoon paprika
¼ teaspoon ground red pepper
2 teaspoons vegetable oil
1 pound mesquite marinated chicken breasts,
    cut into bite-size pieces

1. Cook pasta according to package directions, omitting salt. Drain; set aside.

2. Combine chili powder, cumin, paprika and red pepper in small bowl; set aside.

3. Heat oil in large nonstick skillet over medium-high heat until hot. Add chili powder mixture; cook 30 seconds, stirring constantly. Add chicken; cook and stir 5 to 6 minutes or until cooked through and lightly browned. Add pasta to skillet; stir. Cook 1 to 2 minutes or until heated through. Sprinkle with additional chili powder, if desired. *Makes 4 servings*

Fix It *Fast*

A pasta pot with a perforated insert eliminates the need to carry a heavy pot of boiling water to the sink to drain the pasta. Just lift out the insert with the cooked pasta to drain off the water. Then set the insert on a plate or pan to catch the drips.

Spicy Mesquite Chicken Fettuccine

CHICKEN AND TOMATOES IN RED PEPPER CREAM

9 ounces fresh angel hair pasta
1 jar (7 ounces) roasted red peppers, drained
⅓ cup half-and-half
2 teaspoons Dijon mustard
1 teaspoon salt
12 sun-dried tomatoes (packed in oil), drained
1 tablespoon olive oil
4 boneless skinless chicken breasts (about 1 pound)
  Black pepper
  Grated Parmesan cheese

1. Cook pasta according to package directions; drain.

2. While pasta is cooking, combine red peppers, half-and-half, mustard and salt in food processor or blender; cover and process until smooth. Set aside.

3. Rinse tomatoes in warm water; drain and pat dry. Cut in half.

4. Heat olive oil in large skillet over medium-high heat until hot. Add chicken and tomatoes; sprinkle with pepper. Cook chicken, uncovered, 3 minutes per side.

5. Add red pepper mixture. Cook 3 minutes or until sauce thickens slightly and chicken is no longer pink in center.

6. Serve chicken and sauce over pasta. Sprinkle with Parmesan cheese.   *Makes 4 servings*

Prep and Cook Time: 15 minutes

Chicken and Tomatoes in Red Pepper Cream

DRESSED CHICKEN BREASTS WITH ANGEL HAIR PASTA

1 cup prepared HIDDEN VALLEY® The Original Ranch® Dressing
⅓ cup Dijon-style mustard
4 whole chicken breasts, halved, skinned, boned and pounded thin
½ cup butter or margarine
⅓ cup dry white wine
10 ounces angel hair pasta, cooked and drained
Chopped parsley

In small bowl, whisk together salad dressing and mustard; set aside. In medium skillet, sauté chicken in butter until browned; transfer to dish. Keep warm. Pour wine into skillet; cook over medium-high heat, scraping up any browned bits from bottom of skillet, about 5 minutes. Whisk in dressing mixture; blend well. Serve chicken with sauce over pasta; sprinkle with parsley. *Makes 8 servings*

CHICKEN DIJON WITH SPINACH

1 pound boneless skinless chicken cutlets
2 cloves garlic, minced
¾ cup chicken broth
¼ cup *French's*® Honey Dijon Mustard
2 cups fresh spinach, washed and torn
⅓ cup heavy cream
1 package (9 ounces) fresh linguine pasta, cooked

1. Heat *1 tablespoon oil* in large nonstick skillet over high heat. Add chicken; cook 5 minutes or until browned on both sides. Add garlic; cook and stir just until golden.

2. Combine broth and mustard. Pour over chicken. Heat to boiling. Reduce heat to medium-low. Cook 5 minutes or until chicken is no longer pink in center.

3. Stir in spinach and cream. Heat to boiling. Cook 1 minute or until slightly thickened and spinach wilts. Serve over linguine. Garnish with minced parsley, if desired. *Makes 4 servings*

Dressed Chicken Breast with Angel Hair Pasta

PENNE WITH ROASTED CHICKEN & VEGETABLES

1 whole roasted chicken (about 2 pounds)
1 box (16 ounces) penne pasta
1 pound roasted vegetables, cut into bite-size pieces
⅓ cup shredded Parmesan cheese
Freshly ground black pepper

1. Remove chicken meat from bones and shred. Discard bones and skin.

2. Cook pasta according to package directions; drain and return to hot cooking pot. Add chicken and vegetables; toss together until dish is heated through. Sprinkle with cheese and season with pepper to taste.   *Makes 6 servings*

FIX IT
Fast

Cook twice as much pasta as you need one night and get a head start on the next pasta meal. Thoroughly drain the pasta you are not using immediately and plunge it into a bowl of ice water to stop the cooking. Drain completely and toss with 1 or 2 tablespoons of olive oil. Cover and refrigerate up to 3 days. To reheat the pasta, microwave on HIGH for 2 to 4 minutes, stirring once.

Penne with Roasted Chicken & Vegetables

CHICKEN CACCIATORE

8 ounces uncooked pasta
1 can (15 ounces) chunky Italian-style tomato sauce
1 cup sliced onion
1 cup sliced mushrooms
1 cup chopped green bell pepper
   Nonstick cooking spray
4 boneless skinless chicken breasts (about 1 pound)
   Salt and pepper

1. Cook pasta according to package directions; drain.

2. While pasta is cooking, combine tomato sauce, onion, mushrooms and bell pepper in microwavable dish. Cover loosely with plastic wrap or waxed paper; microwave on HIGH 6 to 8 minutes, stirring halfway through cooking time.

3. Meanwhile, coat large skillet with cooking spray; heat over medium-high heat. Cook chicken breasts 3 to 4 minutes per side or until lightly browned.

4. Add sauce mixture to skillet; season with salt and pepper. Reduce heat to medium and simmer 12 to 15 minutes. Serve over pasta.

Makes 4 servings

Prep and Cook Time: 30 minutes

FIX IT *Fast*

To test the doneness of pasta, cook the pasta for the minimum time specified on the package. Remove a noodle and run it briefly under cold water. Bite into the noodle. It should be cooked through with no hard, opaque core, but not too mushy.

Chicken Cacciatore

HONEY MUSTARD BBQ CHICKEN STIR-FRY

1 box (10 ounces) couscous pasta
1 pound boneless skinless chicken, cut into strips
1 medium red bell pepper, cut into thin strips
1 medium onion, sliced
⅓ cup *French's*® Sweet & Tangy Honey Mustard
⅓ cup barbecue sauce

1. Prepare couscous according to package directions. Keep warm. Heat *1 tablespoon oil* in large nonstick skillet over medium-high heat. Cook and stir chicken in batches 5 to 10 minutes or until browned. Transfer to bowl. Drain fat.

2. Heat *1 tablespoon oil* in same skillet until hot. Cook and stir vegetables 3 minutes or until crisp-tender. Return chicken to skillet. Stir in ⅔ *cup water*, mustard and barbecue sauce. Heat to boiling, stirring often. Serve over couscous. *Makes 4 servings*

CHICKEN CARBONARA

1 pound chicken tenders
1 jar (12 ounces) Alfredo sauce
1 cup milk
1⅓ cups *French's*® French Fried Onions, divided
½ of a 10-ounce package frozen peas, thawed and drained
2 tablespoons real bacon bits *or* 2 strips crumbled crisp-cooked bacon
Hot cooked pasta

1. Spray large nonstick skillet with nonstick cooking spray; heat over high heat. Add chicken; cook and stir about 5 minutes or until browned.

2. Stir in Alfredo sauce and milk. Add ⅔ cup French Fried Onions, peas and bacon bits. Bring to a boil. Reduce heat to low. Cook 5 minutes, stirring occasionally. Serve over pasta. Sprinkle with remaining ⅔ cup onions. *Makes 4 to 6 servings*

Honey Mustard BBQ Chicken Stir-Fry

SUPER SPEEDY CHICKEN ON ANGEL HAIR PASTA

1 package (12 ounces) angel hair pasta
3 boneless skinless chicken breasts (12 ounces)
2 cups baby carrots
1 tablespoon olive oil
2 cups broccoli florets
¼ cup water
1 teaspoon instant chicken bouillon granules
1 jar (28 ounces) chunky-style pasta sauce
⅓ cup grated Parmesan cheese

1. Cook pasta according to package directions.

2. Meanwhile, cut chicken into 1-inch cubes. Cut carrots in half lengthwise.

3. Heat oil in large nonstick skillet over medium heat. Add chicken; cook and stir 5 minutes. Stir in carrots, broccoli, water and chicken bouillon. Reduce heat to low; cover and cook 5 minutes or until vegetables are crisp-tender.

4. Bring pasta sauce to a boil in medium saucepan over high heat. Place pasta on plates; top with hot pasta sauce and chicken mixture. Sprinkle with cheese.   *Makes 6 servings*

Prep and Cook Time: 25 minutes

Super Speedy Chicken on Angel Hair Pasta

RUSTIC DIJON CHICKEN WITH TOMATO PESTO

1 tablespoon olive oil
1 teaspoon minced garlic
4 boneless skinless chicken breast halves (1 pound)
1 can (14½ ounces) diced tomatoes or crushed tomatoes
    in purée, undrained
1 container (4 ounces) prepared pesto sauce
1⅓ cups *French's®* French Fried Onions, divided
2 tablespoons *French's®* Honey Dijon Mustard
   Hot cooked noodles or pasta

1. Heat oil in 12-inch nonstick skillet over medium-high heat. Add garlic; sauté 30 seconds. Add chicken; sauté 5 minutes or until chicken is browned on both sides.

2. Add tomatoes with juice, pesto sauce, *1 cup* French Fried Onions and mustard. Reduce heat to medium-low. Simmer 5 minutes or until chicken is no longer pink in center and sauce thickens slightly.

3. To serve, arrange chicken over hot cooked noodles or pasta. Top with sauce and sprinkle with remaining onions.

Makes 4 servings

Prep Time: 5 minutes
Cook Time: about 10 minutes

Rustic Dijon Chicken with Tomato Pesto

CHICKEN & CREAMY GARLIC SAUCE

1 teaspoon olive oil
4 boneless, skinless chicken breast halves
1 jar (1 pound) RAGÚ® Cheesy! Roasted Garlic Parmesan Sauce
1 small tomato, chopped
8 ounces rotelle pasta, cooked and drained
Crumbled bacon and chopped fresh basil (optional)

In 12-inch nonstick skillet, heat olive oil over medium heat and lightly brown chicken. Stir in Ragú Cheesy! Roasted Garlic Parmesan Sauce and tomato. Simmer covered, stirring occasionally, 10 minutes or until chicken is thoroughly cooked. To serve, spoon chicken and sauce over hot pasta. Garnish, if desired, with crisp-cooked crumbled bacon and chopped fresh basil.

Makes 4 servings

SANTA FE CHICKEN & PASTA

1 jar (12 ounces) mild chunky salsa
1 can (10¾ ounces) condensed Cheddar cheese soup
¾ cup sour cream
5 cups hot cooked ziti pasta (8 ounces uncooked)
1⅓ cups *French's*® French Fried Onions, divided
1 package (10 ounces) fully cooked carved chicken breast (2 cups cut-up chicken)
1 cup (4 ounces) cubed Monterey Jack cheese with jalapeño

1. Preheat oven to 375°F. In large bowl, mix salsa, soup and sour cream. Stir in pasta, *⅔ cup* French Fried Onions, chicken and cheese; mix well. Spoon into 3-quart casserole.

2. Cover; bake 40 minutes or until hot and bubbly. Stir.

3. Sprinkle with remaining *⅔ cup* onions. Bake 3 minutes or until onions are golden.

Makes 8 servings

Prep Time: 10 minutes
Cook Time: 43 minutes

Chicken & Creamy Garlic Sauce

COQ AU VIN & PASTA

**4 large or 8 small chicken thighs (2 to 2½ pounds),
    trimmed of excess fat**
2 teaspoons rotisserie or herb chicken seasoning*
1 tablespoon margarine or butter
3 cups (8 ounces) halved or quartered mushrooms
1 medium onion, coarsely chopped
½ cup dry white wine or vermouth
1 (4.9-ounce) package PASTA RONI® Homestyle Chicken Flavor
½ cup sliced green onions

*1 teaspoon paprika and 1 teaspoon garlic salt can be substituted.

1. Sprinkle meaty side of chicken with rotisserie seasoning. In large skillet over medium-high heat, melt margarine. Add chicken, seasoned-side down; cook 3 minutes. Reduce heat to medium-low; turn chicken over.

2. Add mushrooms, onion and wine. Cover; simmer 15 to 18 minutes or until chicken is no longer pink inside. Remove chicken from skillet; set aside.

3. In same skillet, bring 1 cup water to a boil. Stir in pasta, green onions and Special Seasonings. Place chicken over pasta. Reduce heat to medium-low. Cover; gently boil 6 to 8 minutes or until pasta is tender. Let stand 3 to 5 minutes before serving.

Makes 4 servings

Prep Time: 10 minutes
Cook Time: 30 minutes

Coq au Vin & Pasta

CHICKEN ÉTOUFFÉ WITH PASTA

¼ cup vegetable oil
⅓ cup all-purpose flour
½ cup finely chopped onion
4 boneless skinless chicken breasts (about 1 pound),
cut across the grain into ¼-inch-thick strips
1 cup chicken broth
1 medium tomato, chopped
¾ cup sliced celery
1 medium green bell pepper, chopped
2 teaspoons Creole or Cajun seasoning blend
Hot cooked pasta

1. Heat oil in large skillet over medium heat until hot. Add flour; cook and stir 10 minutes or until dark brown. Add onion; cook and stir 2 minutes.

2. Stir in chicken, broth, tomato, celery, bell pepper and seasoning blend. Cook 8 minutes or until chicken is cooked through. Serve over pasta. *Makes 6 servings*

Prep and Cook Time: 25 minutes

FIX IT *Fast*

Étouffé is a popular Cajun dish from New Orleans. This thick spicy stew usually features chicken or shellfish, bell peppers, onions and celery. The flavor comes from the brown flour mixture that thickens the stew.

Chicken Étouffé with Pasta

CHICKEN AND LINGUINE IN CREAMY TOMATO SAUCE

1 tablespoon olive oil
1 pound boneless, skinless chicken breasts,
    cut into ½-inch strips
1 jar (1 pound 10 ounces) RAGÚ® Old World Style®
    Pasta Sauce
2 cups water
8 ounces uncooked linguine or spaghetti
½ cup whipping or heavy cream
1 tablespoon chopped fresh basil leaves
    or ½ teaspoon dried basil leaves, crushed

1. In 12-inch skillet, heat olive oil over medium heat and brown chicken. Remove chicken and set aside.

2. In same skillet, stir in Ragú Pasta Sauce and water. Bring to a boil over high heat. Stir in uncooked linguine and return to a boil. Reduce heat to low and simmer covered, stirring occasionally, 15 minutes or until linguine is tender.

3. Stir in cream and basil. Return chicken to skillet and cook 5 minutes or until chicken is thoroughly cooked.

Makes 4 servings

Prep Time: 10 minutes
Cook Time: 30 minutes

FIX IT *Fast*

Refrigerated pasta is perfect for fast meals because it cooks in less than half the time needed for dry pasta. However, take care not to overcook the pasta or it can easily become mushy.

Chicken and Linguine in Creamy Tomato Sauce

Chicken Pesto Mozzarella

6 to 8 ounces linguine or corkscrew pasta
4 boneless, skinless chicken breasts
1 tablespoon olive oil
1 can (14½ ounces) DEL MONTE® Diced Tomatoes with Basil,
  Garlic & Oregano
½ medium onion, chopped
⅓ cup sliced ripe olives
 4 teaspoons pesto sauce*
¼ cup (1 ounce) shredded mozzarella cheese

Pesto sauce is available frozen or refrigerated at the supermarket.

1. Cook pasta according to package directions; drain.

2. Meanwhile, season chicken with salt and pepper, if desired. In large skillet, brown chicken in hot oil over medium-high heat. Add undrained tomatoes, onion and olives; bring to boil. Cover and cook 8 minutes over medium heat.

3. Remove cover; cook about 8 minutes or until chicken is no longer pink in center.

4. Spread 1 teaspoon pesto over each chicken breast; top with cheese. Cover and cook until cheese is melted. Serve over pasta. Garnish, if desired.   *Makes 4 servings*

Prep Time: 10 minutes
Cook Time: 25 minutes

Chicken Pesto Mozzarella

Speedy Salads

Buffalo Chicken Salad Italiano

½ cup *Frank's® RedHot®* Buffalo Wing Sauce
½ cup prepared Italian salad dressing
 1 pound frozen chicken tenders, thawed
 8 cups torn salad greens
 1 cup sliced celery
 1 cup crumbled gorgonzola or blue cheese

1. Combine Wing Sauce and salad dressing in bowl. Pour ½ cup mixture over chicken tenders in large bowl. Cover and refrigerate 20 minutes.

2. Cook chicken on electric grill pan or barbecue grill for 3 to 5 minutes until no longer pink in center.

3. Arrange salad greens, celery and cheese on serving plates. Top with chicken and drizzle with remaining Wing Sauce mixture.   *Makes 4 servings*

Tip: You may substitute 1 pound boneless, skinless chicken breast halves for chicken tenders.

Prep Time: 5 minutes
Cook Time: 5 minutes
Marinate Time: 20 minutes

CHICKEN CAESAR SALAD

6 ounces chicken breast tenders
¼ cup plus 1 tablespoon Caesar salad dressing, divided
Black pepper
4 cups (about 5 ounces) prepared Italian salad mix (romaine and radicchio)
½ cup prepared croutons, divided
2 tablespoons grated Parmesan cheese

1. Cut chicken in half lengthwise and crosswise. Heat 1 tablespoon salad dressing in large nonstick skillet. Add chicken; cook and stir over medium heat 3 to 4 minutes or until chicken is cooked through. Remove chicken from skillet; sprinkle with pepper and let cool.

2. Combine salad mix, half of croutons, remaining ¼ cup salad dressing and Parmesan in serving bowl; toss to coat. Top with remaining croutons and chicken. *Makes 2 servings*

Prep and Cook Time: 17 minutes

PINEAPPLE CHICKEN SALAD

1 packet (1 ounce) HIDDEN VALLEY® The Original Ranch® Salad Dressing & Seasoning Mix
½ cup mayonnaise
¼ cup pineapple juice
2 cups cubed, cooked chicken
1 cup sliced celery
1 can (20 ounces) pineapple chunks (reserve juice for above)

Combine salad dressing & seasoning mix with mayonnaise and pineapple juice. Add chicken, celery and pineapple to mixture and toss well to coat. Chill. *Makes 4 to 6 servings*

Chicken Caesar Salad

FINGER-LICKIN' CHICKEN SALAD

½ **cup diced roasted skinless chicken**
½ **rib celery, cut into 1-inch pieces**
¼ **cup drained mandarin orange segments**
¼ **cup red seedless grapes**
 2 **tablespoons lemon yogurt**
 1 **tablespoon mayonnaise**
¼ **teaspoon soy sauce**
⅛ **teaspoon pumpkin pie spice or cinnamon**

1. Toss together chicken, celery, oranges and grapes in plastic container; cover.

2. For dipping sauce, combine yogurt, mayonnaise, soy sauce and pumpkin pie spice in small bowl. Place in small plastic container; cover.

3. Pack chicken mixture and dipping sauce in insulated bag with ice pack. To serve, dip chicken mixture into dipping sauce.

Makes 1 serving

FIX IT *Fast*

For variety, replace the mandarin oranges and grapes with toasted pecans and pineapple chunks.

Finger-Lickin' Chicken Salad

OUTRAGEOUS MEXICAN CHICKEN SALAD

6 cups shredded lettuce
1 bag (9 ounces) tortilla chips, crushed (about 3 cups)
2 cups cubed cooked chicken
1 can (15½ ounces) kidney beans, rinsed and drained
1½ cups prepared HIDDEN VALLEY® The Original Ranch® Dressing
½ cup (2 ounces) shredded Cheddar cheese
   Tomatoes and olives

Combine lettuce, tortilla chips, chicken, beans, dressing and cheese in a large bowl. Garnish with tomatoes and olives.

Makes 4 to 6 servings

CHICKEN AND VEGETABLE STIR-FRY SALAD

1 DOLE® Red or Green Bell Pepper, cut into squares
6 ounces fresh portobella mushrooms or large button mushrooms, coarsely chopped
2 tablespoons olive or vegetable oil
1 package (6 ounces) precooked chicken strips
1 package (8 to 12 ounces) DOLE® Special Blends Salad, any variety
½ cup French or catalina salad dressing, divided

• Stir bell pepper and mushrooms in hot oil in large skillet. Cook 5 minutes or until vegetables are tender crisp. Carefully stir in chicken; heat through. Remove from heat; cool slightly before adding to salad.

• Combine salad blend in large bowl; pour ¼ cup dressing over salad. Toss to evenly coat.

• Line 4 individual plates with salad. Arrange chicken mixture over salad; pour remaining ¼ cup dressing over chicken. Toss to evenly coat.

Makes 4 servings

Outrageous Mexican Chicken Salad

HULA CHICKEN SALAD WITH ORANGE POPPY SEED DRESSING

½ cup prepared vinaigrette salad dressing
¼ cup *French's®* Honey Dijon Mustard
1 tablespoon grated orange peel
1 tablespoon water
1 teaspoon poppy seeds
1 pound chicken tenders
1 tablespoon jerk seasoning
8 cups cut-up romaine lettuce
3 cups cut-up fruit from salad bar such as oranges, melon, strawberries, pineapple

1. Combine salad dressing, mustard, orange peel, water and poppy seeds; mix well. Reserve.

2. Rub chicken tenders with jerk seasoning. Skewer chicken and grill over medium-high heat until no longer pink, about 5 minutes per side.

3. Arrange lettuce and fruit on salad plates. Top with chicken and serve with dressing. *Makes 4 servings*

Tip: To reduce carbs further, use 3 cups strawberries for 13g net carbs.

Prep Time: 15 minutes
Cook Time: 10 minutes

FIX IT *Fast*

If you don't have jerk seasoning, combine 1½ teaspoons each salt and ground allspice; 1 teaspoon each sugar, dried thyme and black pepper; ½ teaspoon each garlic powder and ground red pepper; and ¼ teaspoon each ground cinnamon and ground nutmeg.

Hula Chicken Salad with Orange Poppy Seed Dressing

WARM CHUTNEY CHICKEN SALAD

Nonstick olive oil cooking spray
6 ounces boneless skinless chicken breasts, cut into bite-size pieces
⅓ cup mango chutney
¼ cup water
1 tablespoon Dijon mustard
4 cups packaged mixed salad greens
1 cup chopped peeled mango or papaya
Sliced green onions

1. Spray medium nonstick skillet with cooking spray. Heat over medium-high heat. Add chicken; cook and stir 2 to 3 minutes or until cooked through. Stir in chutney, water and mustard. Cook and stir just until hot. Cool slightly.

2. Toss together salad greens and mango. Arrange on serving plates.

3. Spoon chicken mixture onto greens. Garnish with green onions.

Makes 2 servings

GRILLED CHICKEN WITH PEAR & WALNUT SALAD

4 boneless, skinless chicken breast halves, grilled or broiled
3 cups torn green leaf and/or romaine lettuce
2 medium red pears or apples, cored and cut into thin wedges
¼ cup chopped walnuts, toasted
¼ cup WISH-BONE® Chunky Blue Cheese or Just 2 Good! Chunky Blue Cheese Dressing

Season chicken, if desired, with salt and pepper; set aside.

In large bowl, combine all ingredients except chicken. On platter, arrange salad. Top with chicken. Serve immediately.

Makes about 4 servings

Prep Time: 25 minutes

Warm Chutney Chicken Salad

CURRIED PASTA SALAD

4 ounces uncooked bow tie or corkscrew (fusilli) pasta
1 can (8 ounces) DOLE® Pineapple Chunks
½ cup fat free or reduced fat mayonnaise
2 teaspoons packed brown sugar
1 teaspoon curry powder
1 can (11 or 15 ounces) DOLE® Mandarin Oranges, drained
1½ cups cooked chicken breast or turkey breast strips
½ cup sliced celery
¼ cup chopped green onions

• Cook pasta as package directs; drain.

• Drain pineapple chunks, reserving 3 tablespoons juice.

• Stir reserved juice, mayonnaise, sugar and curry in large serving bowl until blended.

• Add pasta, pineapple chunks, mandarin oranges, chicken, celery and green onions to curry dressing; toss to evenly coat. Serve on lettuce-lined plate and garnish with shredded red cabbage, if desired.

Makes 4 servings

Prep Time: 10 minutes
Cook Time: 15 minutes

 FIX IT *Fast*

Do not rinse pasta since it removes the excess starch and keeps the pasta from sticking together.

Curried Pasta Salad

COBB SALAD

1 package (10 ounces) torn mixed salad greens
   or 8 cups torn romaine lettuce
6 ounces deli chicken, turkey or smoked turkey breast,
   cut ¼ inch thick
1 large tomato, seeded and chopped
⅓ cup bacon bits or crisp-cooked bacon, crumbled
1 large ripe avocado, peeled and diced
⅓ cup prepared blue cheese or Caesar salad dressing

1. Place lettuce in salad bowl.

2. Dice chicken; place in center of lettuce.

3. Arrange tomato, bacon and avocado in rows on either side of chicken.

4. Drizzle with dressing. Serve immediately.   *Makes 4 servings*

Serving suggestion: Serve with warm French or Italian rolls.

Prep Time: 15 minutes

WALDORF CHICKEN SALAD

⅓ cup plain yogurt
⅓ cup mayonnaise or salad dressing
2 tablespoons frozen orange juice concentrate, thawed
¼ teaspoon each salt and pepper
2 (10-ounce) cans HORMEL® chunk breast of chicken,
   drained and flaked
1 apple, diced
1 cup sliced celery
½ cup halved grapes
½ cup chopped pecans or walnuts, toasted

In small bowl, combine yogurt, mayonnaise, orange juice, salt and pepper; mix well. In large bowl, combine chunk chicken, apple, celery, grapes and nuts. Add dressing; toss to coat.   *Makes 6 servings*

Speedy Salads

Cobb Salad

Effortless
Sandwiches

ASIAN WRAPS

Nonstick cooking spray
8 ounces boneless skinless chicken breasts or thighs,
    cut into ½-inch pieces
1 teaspoon minced fresh ginger
1 teaspoon minced fresh garlic
¼ teaspoon red pepper flakes
¼ cup teriyaki sauce
4 cups (about 8 ounces) packaged coleslaw mix
½ cup sliced green onions
4 (10-inch) flour tortillas
8 teaspoons plum fruit spread

1. Spray nonstick wok or large skillet with cooking spray;
heat over medium-high heat. Stir-fry chicken 2 minutes. Add
ginger, garlic and pepper flakes; stir-fry 2 minutes. Add
teriyaki sauce; mix well.* Add coleslaw mix and onions;
stir-fry 4 minutes or until chicken is cooked through and
cabbage is crisp-tender.

2. Spread each tortilla with 2 teaspoons fruit spread; evenly
spoon chicken mixture down center of tortillas. Roll up to
form wraps.   *Makes 4 servings*

*If sauce is too thick, add up to 2 tablespoons water to thin it.

Prep Time: 10 minutes
Cook Time: 10 minutes

GLAZED TERIYAKI CHICKEN STIR-FRY SUB

¼ cup *French's®* Honey Dijon Mustard
2 tablespoons teriyaki sauce
1 tablespoon sucralose sugar substitute
1 tablespoon grated, peeled ginger root
1 tablespoon cider or red wine vinegar
1 tablespoon vegetable oil
1 pound boneless skinless chicken, cut into thin strips
1 cup coarsely chopped red or yellow bell peppers
½ cup each coarsely chopped red onion and plum tomatoes
2 cups shredded Napa cabbage or romaine lettuce
4 Italian hero rolls, split (about 8 inches each)

1. Combine mustard, teriyaki sauce, sugar substitute, ginger and vinegar in small bowl; set aside.

2. Heat oil in large skillet or wok over high heat. Stir-fry chicken 5 minutes until no longer pink. Add vegetables and stir-fry 2 minutes until just tender. Pour sauce mixture over stir-fry and cook 1 minute.

3. Arrange cabbage on rolls and top with equal portions of stir-fry. Close rolls. Serve warm.   *Makes 4 servings*

Low-Carb Tip: To reduce carbs to 10g net per serving, omit rolls and serve on shredded Napa cabbage.

Tip: If desired, substitute 1 pound sliced boneless pork or steak for the chicken.

Prep Time: 10 minutes
Cook Time: 8 minutes

Glazed Teriyaki Chicken Stir-Fry Sub

SPICY CHICKEN STROMBOLI

1 cup frozen broccoli florets, thawed
1 can (10 ounces) diced chicken
1½ cups (6 ounces) shredded Monterey Jack cheese
　　with jalapeño peppers
¼ cup chunky salsa
2 green onions, chopped
1 can (10 ounces) refrigerated pizza dough

1. Preheat oven to 400°F. Coarsely chop broccoli. Combine broccoli, chicken, cheese, salsa and onions in small bowl.

2. Unroll pizza dough. Pat into 15×10-inch rectangle. Sprinkle broccoli mixture evenly over top. Starting with long side, tightly roll into log jelly-roll style. Pinch seam to seal. Place on baking sheet, seam side down.

3. Bake 15 to 20 minutes or until golden brown. Transfer to wire rack to cool slightly. Slice and serve warm.   *Makes 6 servings*

Serving Suggestion: Serve with salsa on the side for dipping or pour salsa on top of slices for a boost of added flavor.

Prep and Cook Time: 30 minutes

FIX IT *Fast*   *A stromboli is a sandwich filled with meat and cheese and wrapped in pizza dough before it is baked.*

Spicy Chicken Stromboli

CHICKEN, FETA AND PEPPER SUBS

1 pound boneless, skinless chicken breasts
3 tablespoons olive oil, divided
2 teaspoons TABASCO® brand Pepper Sauce
½ teaspoon salt
½ teaspoon ground cumin
1 red bell pepper, cut into strips
1 yellow or green bell pepper, cut into strips
½ cup crumbled feta cheese
4 (6-inch) French rolls

Cut chicken breasts into thin strips. Heat 1 tablespoon oil in 12-inch skillet over medium-high heat. Add chicken; cook until well browned on all sides, stirring frequently. Stir in TABASCO® Sauce, salt and cumin. Remove mixture to medium bowl. Add remaining 2 tablespoons oil to same skillet over medium heat. Add bell peppers; cook about 5 minutes or until tender-crisp, stirring occasionally. Toss with chicken and feta cheese.

To serve, cut rolls crosswise in half. Cover bottom halves with chicken mixture and top with remaining roll halves.

Makes 4 servings

FIX IT *Fast*

To easily cut chicken breasts into thin strips, slice the chicken across the grain when partially thawed or partially freeze fresh chicken before slicing.

Chicken, Feta and Pepper Sub

OPEN-FACED ITALIAN FOCACCIA SANDWICH

2 cups shredded cooked chicken
½ cup HIDDEN VALLEY® The Original Ranch® Dressing
¼ cup diagonally sliced green onions
1 piece focaccia bread, about ¾-inch thick, 10×7-inches
2 medium tomatoes, thinly sliced
4 cheese slices, such as provolone, Cheddar or Swiss
2 tablespoons grated Parmesan cheese (optional)

Stir together chicken, dressing and onions in a small mixing bowl. Arrange chicken mixture evenly on top of focaccia. Top with layer of tomatoes and cheese slices. Sprinkle with Parmesan cheese, if desired. Broil 2 minutes or until cheese is melted and bubbly.

Makes 4 servings

Note: Purchase rotisserie chicken at your favorite store to add great taste and save preparation time.

CHICKEN CAESAR SALAD WRAP

1 (10-ounce) can HORMEL® chunk breast of chicken,
    drained and flaked
2 cups thinly sliced Romaine lettuce
1 medium tomato, diced
¼ cup creamy Caesar salad dressing
1 tablespoon grated Parmesan cheese
4 (8-inch) flour tortillas (plain or flavored)

In bowl, combine chicken, lettuce, tomato, salad dressing and Parmesan cheese. Toss until well combined. Evenly divide mixture among each tortilla. Wrap tortillas around filling and serve.

Makes 4 servings

Open-Faced Italian Focaccia Sandwich

MEDITERRANEAN GRILLED CHICKEN WRAPS

½ cup *French's® Gourmayo™* Sun Dried Tomato Light Mayonnaise
1 package (4 ounces) goat cheese, at room temperature
½ cup chopped Spanish olives
5 (10-inch) flour tortillas
2½ cups shredded romaine lettuce
1 pound boneless, skinless chicken breasts; grilled and cut into strips

1. Combine mayonnaise and goat cheese; beat or whisk until smooth. Stir in olives.

2. Spread about 3 tablespoons cheese mixture evenly on each tortilla. Top with lettuce and chicken, dividing evenly. Roll up tightly. Cut in half to serve.   *Makes 5 servings*

CHICKEN LUNCHEON SANDWICH

1½ cups chopped cooked chicken
1 cup (4 ounces) shredded Wisconsin Cheddar cheese
½ cup finely chopped celery
¼ cup chopped green bell pepper
1 green onion, chopped
1 tablespoon chopped pimiento
½ cup mayonnaise
½ cup plain yogurt
Salt and pepper to taste
Rolls or bread
Lettuce leaves

Combine chicken, cheese, celery, bell pepper, onion, pimiento, mayonnaise and yogurt in large bowl. Season with salt and pepper. Stir until well blended. Refrigerate until ready to use. Serve on rolls with lettuce.   *Makes about 5 to 6 servings*

*Favorite recipe from **Wisconsin Milk Marketing Board***

Mediterranean Grilled Chicken Wraps

CHICKEN PARMESAN HERO SANDWICHES

4 boneless, skinless chicken breast halves (about 1¼ pounds)
1 egg, lightly beaten
¾ cup Italian seasoned dry bread crumbs
1 jar (1 pound 10 ounces) RAGÚ® Old World Style® Pasta Sauce
1 cup shredded mozzarella cheese (about 4 ounces)
4 long Italian rolls, halved lengthwise

1. Preheat oven to 400°F. Dip chicken in egg, then bread crumbs, coating well.

2. In 13×9-inch glass baking dish, arrange chicken. Bake uncovered 20 minutes.

3. Pour Ragú Pasta Sauce over chicken, then top with cheese. Bake an additional 10 minutes or until chicken is thoroughly cooked. To serve, arrange chicken and sauce on rolls.   *Makes 4 servings*

GUACAMOLE CHICKEN WRAP

4 (10-inch) flour tortillas
½ cup prepared guacamole
1 package (10 ounces) fully cooked carved chicken breast*
¼ cup *French's*® Bold n' Spicy Brown Mustard
1 tablespoon minced cilantro (optional)
1 cup (4 ounces) shredded Monterey Jack cheese
1 cup shredded lettuce
1 small tomato, chopped

*Or about 2 cups cooked, shredded chicken.

1. Spread each tortilla with *2 tablespoons* guacamole. Toss chicken with mustard and cilantro in medium bowl. Arrange on top of tortillas, dividing evenly. Sprinkle with cheese, lettuce and tomato.

2. Roll up tortillas jelly-roll style. Secure with toothpicks. Microwave on HIGH 3 minutes or until heated through and cheese is melted. Remove toothpicks. Cut in half to serve.   *Makes 4 servings*

Chicken Parmesan Hero Sandwich

TROPICAL CHICKEN SALAD POCKETS

3 cups diced cooked chicken*
1 can (20 ounces) pineapple chunks in juice, drained,
    juice reserved
3 green onions, thinly sliced
2 tablespoons chopped fresh cilantro
    Tropical Dressing (recipe follows)
4 pocket breads, slit
    Lettuce leaves

*Use home-roasted chicken, or ready-to-eat roasted chicken from the supermarket or deli.

In bowl, place chicken, pineapple, green onions, and cilantro. Pour dressing over chicken mixture and toss to mix. Line each pocket bread with lettuce leaf; fill with chicken salad.   *Makes 4 servings*

Tropical Dressing: In small bowl, mix together ½ cup reduced-fat mayonnaise, 1 tablespoon lime juice, 1 tablespoon reserved pineapple juice, 1 teaspoon sugar, 1 teaspoon curry powder, ½ teaspoon salt, and ¼ teaspoon grated lime peel. Makes about ⅔ cup dressing.

Favorite recipe from Delmarva Poultry Industry, Inc.

FIX IT *Fast*

When a recipe calls for chopped cooked chicken, it can be difficult to judge how much chicken to purchase. As a guideline, 2 whole chicken breasts (about 10 ounces each) or 4 halves will yield about 2 cups of chopped cooked chicken; one broiling/frying chicken (about 3 pounds) will yield about 2½ cups chopped cooked chicken.

Tropical Chicken Salad Pockets

Simple Soups

BLACK AND WHITE CHILI

Nonstick cooking spray
1 pound chicken breast tenders, cut into ¾-inch pieces
1 cup coarsely chopped onion
1 can (15½ ounces) Great Northern beans, rinsed
    and drained
1 can (15 ounces) black beans, rinsed and drained
1 can (14½ ounces) Mexican-style stewed tomatoes,
    undrained
2 tablespoons Texas-style chili powder seasoning mix

1. Spray large saucepan with cooking spray; heat over medium heat until hot. Add chicken and onion; cook and stir over medium to medium-high heat 5 to 8 minutes or until chicken is browned.

2. Stir beans, tomatoes with juice and seasoning mix into saucepan; bring to a boil. Reduce heat to low; simmer, uncovered, 10 minutes.   *Makes 6 servings*

Serving Suggestion: For a change of pace, this delicious chili is excellent served over cooked rice or pasta.

Prep and Cook Time: 30 minutes

MEXICALI CHICKEN STEW

1 package (1¼ ounces) taco seasoning, divided
12 ounces boneless skinless chicken thighs
    Nonstick cooking spray
2 cans (14½ ounces each) stewed tomatoes with onions,
    celery and green peppers
1 package (10 ounces) frozen corn
1 package (9 ounces) frozen green beans
4 cups tortilla chips

1. Place half of taco seasoning in small bowl. Cut chicken thighs into 1-inch pieces; coat with taco seasoning.

2. Coat large nonstick skillet with cooking spray. Cook and stir chicken 5 minutes over medium heat. Add tomatoes, corn, beans, and remaining taco seasoning; bring to a boil. Reduce heat to medium-low; simmer 10 minutes. Top with tortilla chips before serving.   *Makes 4 servings*

Serving Suggestion: Serve nachos with the stew. Spread tortilla chips on a plate; dot with salsa and sprinkle with cheese. Heat just until the cheese is melted.

Prep and Cook Time: 20 minutes

Mexicali Chicken Stew

CHICKEN GUMBO

3 tablespoons vegetable oil

1 pound boneless skinless chicken breasts, cut into 1-inch pieces

½ pound smoked sausage,* cut into ¾-inch slices

1 bag (16 ounces) BIRDS EYE® frozen Farm Fresh Mixtures Broccoli, Corn and Red Peppers

1 can (14½ ounces) stewed tomatoes

1½ cups water

For a spicy gumbo, use andouille sausage. Any type of kielbasa or turkey kielbasa can also be used.

• Heat oil in large saucepan over high heat. Add chicken and sausage; cook until browned, about 8 minutes.

• Add vegetables, tomatoes and water; bring to boil. Reduce heat to medium; cover and cook 5 to 6 minutes.

Makes 4 to 6 servings

Prep Time: 5 minutes
Cook Time: 20 minutes

SOUTHWESTERN CHICKEN SOUP

4 cups chicken broth

½ cup long-grain rice, uncooked

¼ teaspoon ground cumin

1 cup chopped cooked chicken

½ cup fresh corn kernels (frozen corn kernels may be substituted)

2 tablespoons SONOMA® Dried Tomato Bits

¼ cup fresh lime juice

¼ teaspoon cayenne pepper

Salt, to taste

In large saucepan, bring chicken broth to a boil. Stir in rice and cumin. Cover and cook 15 minutes or until rice is done. Stir in chicken and corn. Cover and bring just to a boil; remove from heat. Stir in tomato bits, lime juice, cayenne and salt.

Makes 4 servings

Chicken Gumbo

Tex-Mex Chicken & Rice Chili

1 package (6.8 ounces) RICE-A-RONI® Spanish Rice
2¾ cups water
2 cups chopped cooked chicken or turkey
1 can (15 or 16 ounces) kidney beans or pinto beans,
    rinsed and drained
1 can (14½ ounces) tomatoes or stewed tomatoes, undrained
1 medium green bell pepper, cut into ½-inch pieces
1½ teaspoons chili powder
1 teaspoon ground cumin
½ cup (2 ounces) shredded Cheddar or Monterey Jack cheese
    (optional)
  Sour cream (optional)
  Chopped cilantro (optional)

1. In 3-quart saucepan, combine rice-vermicelli mix, Special Seasonings, water, chicken, beans, tomatoes, green pepper, chili powder and cumin. Bring to a boil over high heat.

2. Reduce heat to low; simmer, uncovered, about 20 minutes or until rice is tender, stirring occasionally.

3. Top with cheese, sour cream and cilantro, if desired.

Makes 4 servings

Salsa Corn Soup with Chicken

3 quarts chicken broth
2 pounds boneless skinless chicken breasts, cooked and diced
2 packages (10 ounces each) frozen whole kernel corn, thawed
4 jars (11 ounces each) NEWMAN'S OWN® All Natural Salsa
4 large carrots, diced

Bring chicken broth to a boil in Dutch oven. Add chicken, corn, Newman's Own® Salsa and carrots. Bring to a boil. Reduce heat and simmer until carrots are tender. *Makes 8 servings*

Tex-Mex Chicken & Rice Chili

CHICKEN CORN CHOWDER WITH CHEESE

2 tablespoons butter or margarine
⅓ cup chopped celery
⅓ cup chopped red bell pepper
1½ tablespoons all-purpose flour
2 cups milk
1 can (14¾ ounces) cream-style corn
1⅓ cups *French's*® French Fried Onions, divided
1 cup diced cooked chicken
2 tablespoons chopped green chilies
½ cup (2 ounces) shredded Cheddar cheese

1. Melt butter in 3-quart saucepan over medium-high heat. Sauté celery and bell pepper 3 minutes or until crisp-tender. Blend in flour; cook 1 minute, stirring constantly. Gradually stir in milk and corn. Bring to a boil. Reduce heat; simmer 4 minutes or until thickened, stirring frequently.

2. Add ⅔ *cup* French Fried Onions, chicken and chilies. Cook until heated through. Spoon soup into serving bowls; sprinkle with remaining onions and cheese. Splash on *Frank's RedHot* Sauce to taste, if desired.   *Makes 4 servings*

Variation: For added Cheddar flavor, substitute *French's*® **Cheddar French Fried Onions** for the original flavor.

Prep Time: 5 minutes
Cook Time: 10 minutes

Chicken Corn Chowder with Cheese

THAI NOODLE SOUP

1 package (3 ounces) ramen noodles
¾ pound chicken breast tenders
2 cans (about 14 ounces each) chicken broth
¼ cup shredded carrot
¼ cup frozen snow peas
2 tablespoons thinly sliced green onions
½ teaspoon minced garlic
¼ teaspoon ground ginger
3 tablespoons chopped fresh cilantro
½ lime, cut into 4 wedges

1. Break noodles into pieces. Cook noodles according to package directions; discard flavor packet. Drain and set aside.

2. Cut chicken into ½-inch pieces. Combine chicken broth and chicken in large saucepan or Dutch oven; bring to a boil over medium heat. Cook 2 minutes.

3. Add carrot, snow peas, green onions, garlic and ginger. Reduce heat to low; simmer 3 minutes. Add cooked noodles and cilantro; heat through. Serve soup with lime wedges.   *Makes 4 servings*

Prep and Cook Time: 15 minutes

FIX IT
Fast

When making soup ahead of time, store the soup mixture and noodles in separate containers. When ready to serve, heat the soup mixture then add the noodles. Keeping the noodles separate until ready to serve prevents the noodles from becoming mushy.

Thai Noodle Soup

CAJUN CHILI

6 ounces spicy sausage links, sliced
4 boneless, skinless chicken thighs, cut into cubes
1 medium onion, chopped
⅛ teaspoon cayenne pepper
1 can (15 ounces) black-eyed peas or kidney beans, drained
1 can (14½ ounces) DEL MONTE® Diced Tomatoes with Zesty
    Mild Green Chilies
1 medium green bell pepper, chopped

1. Lightly brown sausage in large skillet over medium-high heat. Add chicken, onion and cayenne pepper; cook until browned. Drain.

2. Stir in remaining ingredients. Cook 5 minutes, stirring occasionally. *Makes 4 servings*

Prep and Cook Time: 20 minutes

JIFFY CHICKEN & RICE GUMBO

1 (6.9-ounce) package RICE-A-RONI® Chicken Flavor
1 small green bell pepper, coarsely chopped
2 tablespoons margarine or butter
1 pound boneless, skinless chicken breasts, cut into 1-inch pieces
1 (14½-ounce) can diced tomatoes with garlic and onion,
    undrained
¾ to 1 teaspoon Creole or Cajun seasoning*

*½ teaspoon cayenne pepper, ¼ teaspoon dried oregano and ¼ teaspoon dried thyme can be substituted.

1. In large skillet over medium heat, sauté rice-vermicelli mix and bell pepper with margarine until vermicelli is golden brown.

2. Slowly stir in 2¼ cups water, chicken, tomatoes, Creole seasoning and Special Seasonings; bring to a boil. Reduce heat to low. Cover; simmer 15 to 20 minutes or until rice is tender.
Makes 4 servings

Prep Time: 5 minutes
Cook Time: 30 minutes

Cajun Chili

CHICKEN SOUP PARMIGIANA

3 cups water
½ pound boneless chicken breasts, cut into ½-inch pieces
1 cup chopped fresh tomatoes *or* 1 can (8 ounces) whole peeled
    tomatoes, undrained and chopped
1 cup sliced zucchini or yellow squash
1 envelope LIPTON® Soup Secrets Noodle Soup Mix with Real
    Chicken Broth
½ teaspoon dried oregano leaves (optional)
½ teaspoon LAWRY'S® Garlic Powder with Parsley
½ teaspoon dried basil leaves* (optional)
⅓ cup shredded mozzarella cheese (about 1 ounce)
    Grated Parmesan cheese

Or, use 2 teaspoons chopped fresh basil leaves.

In medium saucepan, combine all ingredients except cheese. Bring
to a boil, then simmer, stirring occasionally, 5 minutes or until
chicken is thoroughly cooked. To serve, spoon into bowls; sprinkle,
if desired, with mozzarella cheese and grated Parmesan cheese.

Makes about 5 cups

Microwave Directions: In 2-quart microwave-safe casserole,
combine all ingredients except zucchini and cheese; stir thoroughly.
Microwave at HIGH 5 minutes, stirring once. Stir in zucchini.
Microwave at HIGH uncovered 11 minutes or until chicken is
thoroughly cooked; stir. Serve as above.

 FIX IT Fast

*Whole chicken breasts weigh about
10 ounces or 5 ounces for each half.
For this recipe use 2 chicken breast
halves or about 1 to 1½ cups cubed
chicken.*

CHICKEN TORTILLA SOUP

1 teaspoon minced garlic
2½ cups chicken broth
1 jar (16 ounces) mild chunky-style salsa
2 cups cooked finely cut-up chicken
1 cup frozen whole kernel corn
1 to 2 tablespoons *Frank's® RedHot®* Original Cayenne
    Pepper Sauce
1 tablespoon chopped fresh cilantro (optional)
1 cup crushed tortilla chips
    Monterey Jack cheese (optional)

1. Heat *1 tablespoon oil* in large saucepan over medium-high heat. Sauté garlic 1 minute or until tender. Add remaining ingredients *except* tortilla chips. Cover; reduce heat to medium-low and simmer 5 minutes.

2. Stir in tortilla chips. Sprinkle with shredded Monterey Jack cheese, if desired. Serve while hot.   *Makes 4 to 6 servings*

Prep Time: 5 minutes
Cook Time: 6 minutes

HEARTY RICE SOUP

1 package LIPTON® Sides Rice & Sauce–Chicken Flavor
2 cups chicken broth
2 cups water
½ cup sliced carrots
½ cup sliced celery
¼ cup sliced green onions
½ cup cut-up cooked chicken

In medium saucepan, combine all ingredients except chicken; bring to a boil. Continue boiling over medium heat, stirring occasionally, 10 minutes. Stir in chicken and heat through.

Makes 6 (1-cup) servings

Acknowledgments

The publisher would like to thank the companies
and organizations listed below for the use of their recipes and
photographs in this publication.

Birds Eye Foods

Delmarva Poultry Industry, Inc.

Del Monte Corporation

Dole Food Company, Inc.

The Golden Grain Company®

Heinz North America

The Hidden Valley® Food Products Company

Hormel Foods, LLC

The Kingsford® Products Co.

MASTERFOODS USA

McIlhenny Company (TABASCO® brand Pepper Sauce)

Mrs. Dash®

Newman's Own, Inc.®

Ortega®, A Division of B&G Foods, Inc.

Perdue Farms Incorporated

Reckitt Benckiser Inc.

Sonoma® Dried Tomatoes

The Sugar Association, Inc.

Unilever Foods North America

Wisconsin Milk Marketing Board

METRIC CONVERSION CHART

VOLUME MEASUREMENTS (dry)

1/8 teaspoon = 0.5 mL
1/4 teaspoon = 1 mL
1/2 teaspoon = 2 mL
3/4 teaspoon = 4 mL
1 teaspoon = 5 mL
1 tablespoon = 15 mL
2 tablespoons = 30 mL
1/4 cup = 60 mL
1/3 cup = 75 mL
1/2 cup = 125 mL
2/3 cup = 150 mL
3/4 cup = 175 mL
1 cup = 250 mL
2 cups = 1 pint = 500 mL
3 cups = 750 mL
4 cups = 1 quart = 1 L

VOLUME MEASUREMENTS (fluid)

1 fluid ounce (2 tablespoons) = 30 mL
4 fluid ounces (1/2 cup) = 125 mL
8 fluid ounces (1 cup) = 250 mL
12 fluid ounces (1 1/2 cups) = 375 mL
16 fluid ounces (2 cups) = 500 mL

WEIGHTS (mass)

1/2 ounce = 15 g
1 ounce = 30 g
3 ounces = 90 g
4 ounces = 120 g
8 ounces = 225 g
10 ounces = 285 g
12 ounces = 360 g
16 ounces = 1 pound = 450 g

DIMENSIONS

1/16 inch = 2 mm
1/8 inch = 3 mm
1/4 inch = 6 mm
1/2 inch = 1.5 cm
3/4 inch = 2 cm
1 inch = 2.5 cm

OVEN TEMPERATURES

250°F = 120°C
275°F = 140°C
300°F = 150°C
325°F = 160°C
350°F = 180°C
375°F = 190°C
400°F = 200°C
425°F = 220°C
450°F = 230°C

BAKING PAN SIZES

Utensil	Size in Inches/Quarts	Metric Volume	Size in Centimeters
Baking or Cake Pan (square or rectangular)	8×8×2	2 L	20×20×5
	9×9×2	2.5 L	23×23×5
	12×8×2	3 L	30×20×5
	13×9×2	3.5 L	33×23×5
Loaf Pan	8×4×3	1.5 L	20×10×7
	9×5×3	2 L	23×13×7
Round Layer Cake Pan	8×1½	1.2 L	20×4
	9×1½	1.5 L	23×4
Pie Plate	8×1¼	750 mL	20×3
	9×1¼	1 L	23×3
Baking Dish or Casserole	1 quart	1 L	—
	1½ quart	1.5 L	—
	2 quart	2 L	—